COMEDY RULES

From the Cambridge Footlights to
Yes Prime Minister

JONATHAN LYNN

faber and faber

First published in 2011
by Faber and Faber Limited
Bloomsbury House
74–77 Great Russell Street, London WC1B 3DA
First published in paperback 2012

A CIP record for this book
is available from the British Library

ISBN 978-0-571-27796-4

2 4 6 8 10 9 7 5 3 1

To Tony Jay
my colleague, mentor and friend

Humor can be dissected as a frog can, but the thing dies in the process and the innards are discouraging to any but the pure scientific mind.

E. B. White

This is not a practical handbook, nor a *How to . . .* book. It is part memoir, with some stories from that part of my life that has been spent, or misspent, making people laugh. Laughter is good for people, but my job is not altruistic; I do it for myself. It is exhilarating, tremendous fun when audiences laugh at what you thought up, and gratifying because their laughter indicates that, at that moment at least, they share or understand your point of view.

I also do it because it's much better than a proper job. I have not had to get a proper job since I sold records at Selfridges at Christmas, 1966, and that makes me very fortunate.

When I was a child I used to think people who wrote comedy had a mysterious, even magical, gift. How do they do it, I wondered? How do they know what will make people laugh, week after week, month after month, year after year? I went to the cinema as often as I could, I watched TV shows that I loved and admired, films starring Abbott and Costello, Laurel and Hardy, Danny Kaye and Cary Grant and Alec Guinness. I, alone among my friends, noticed and memorised the names of the people who had written them: Ray

Galton and Alan Simpson (*Hancock's Half Hour* and *Steptoe and Son*), Carl Reiner (*The Dick Van Dyke Show*), Nat Hiken and Neil Simon (*The Phil Silvers Show*), Norman Panama & Melvin Frank (*The Court Jester*), Donald Ogden Stewart (*The Philadelphia Story*), William Rose (*The Ladykillers*), Robert Hamer (*Kind Hearts and Coronets*), Billy Wilder & I. A. L. Diamond (*The Apartment* and *Some Like It Hot*). My greatest influence was George Bernard Shaw – I saw *Pygmalion* at the Bristol Old Vic, with a twenty-six-year-old Peter O'Toole as Alfred P. Doolittle. Then I read nearly all his plays and prefaces. I wanted to be one of those people who could make everybody laugh. And think.

Nowadays, people ask me the questions I used to ask, and it is hard to find answers. What is the process? What are the tricks of the trade? Why is 'Dying is easy, Comedy is hard' so often quoted? Is comedy really harder than other forms of drama, and, if so, why?

To me, comedy is endlessly fascinating because it is so elusive. This little book makes no attempt to find definitive answers; I am simply reporting what I have learned from my own necessarily limited experience. Students and practitioners of comedy may find it useful, but my hope is that it may help the general reader understand what makes an audience laugh at a play or a film.

There are a large number of rules in these pages, which are true for me and to which more attention should be paid if you are reading the book for the wrong purpose (*How to . . .*). Here is the most important one:

1. There are exceptions to every rule in this book.

Except this one, of course.

***

In 1987 Peter Hall asked me if I would like to have my own company at the National Theatre and do one play in each of the three houses there. Business was not good at the theatre and he wanted me to do three 'box office' shows. I was both flattered and discouraged that I was hired for this purpose: his attitude was that I was in some way 'commercial', a backhanded compliment at the NT. That was because he associated me with comedy.

Tragedies and comedies both say the same thing: terrible things will happen to you, and to society, if you break our rules and taboos. If, like Oedipus, you commit incest, you will suffer and die. This was vitally important to a small city-state like Athens because incest threatens the species.

Similarly, in a marital farce by Georges Feydeau (or a 1930s screwball comedy), if the hero tries to commit adultery, or even have sex outside marriage, he will be exposed and ridiculed. This was important to bourgeois society, which felt threatened by adultery. To be respectable and dignified were society's highest values.

Peter told me that the Cottesloe, the smallest house at the NT, was originally conceived as an experimental theatre, so I proposed what I thought would be a fascinating theatrical experiment, an illustration of something that I had discussed a lot with John Lahr, now drama critic of *The New Yorker*, when I had Feydeau's *A Little Hotel on the Side* at the NT and Joe Orton's *Loot* in the West End, three years earlier:

2. Tragedy and farce are two sides of the same coin.

These are the two elemental forms of theatre. Drama and

comedy lie somewhere in the middle, along the continuum between tragedy and farce. Tragedy is drama at its purest. Farce is comedy at its purest.

Tragedy is a drama in which the protagonist initiates a course of events that will lead inevitably to his own destruction. It is driven by the flaws in the protagonist's own character. A farce has the same structure: in both genres events spin dangerously out of control, leading eventually to madness, usually followed by a measure of understanding and resolution.

If a play is a tragedy, the audience is asked to empathise with the protagonist. If the play is a comedy, the audience is asked to laugh at him.

3. Comedy is objective. Tragedy is subjective.

The structural difference is that, whereas tragedy ends in the death of the protagonist, a farce usually ends in the restoration of the *status quo ante*, reassuring the audience that society's values are still intact and survival is possible once punishment and humiliation have been inflicted.

Some people use the word 'farce' pejoratively. In 1967, when I was playing Motel in the original London cast of *Fiddler on the Roof*, one of the stagehands, Tony, a thin, short man – I'm only five foot six and he was somewhat smaller – told me that every Christmas for several years he had acted in *Peter Pan*. I asked him who he played. 'Nana,' he said.

I had never seen or read *Peter Pan*. 'Who's that?'

'Nana? Don't you know? Nana's the dog.'

'Is it a good part?'

'It's a great part. I've been playing it for nine years.'

'So . . . do you have much to say?'

'To *say*?' Tony was scathing. 'Nana's a *dog*. They think I'm a *dog*. I wear a *dog*-suit.'

'I see,' I said. 'So why is it such a great part, exactly?'

'It's farce. It's pure farce. You just jump around a bit and bark when you feel like it.'

I have always cherished that definition of farce. It is so magnificently wrong.

4. 'Farcical' is not a synonym for 'idiotic', nor for 'chaotic'.

A farce may appear to be both, but it must in fact be tightly controlled and logically built.

5. In all comedy the driving force of the story must be a hideous dilemma for one or more of the characters.

In a film I directed, *My Cousin Vinny*, two young men are arrested and charged with a murder that the audience knows they did not commit. Vinny, a cousin of one of them from New York, is a recently qualified trial lawyer who passed his bar finals at his sixth attempt. He has never taken part in a trial. He arrives in Alabama, a death-penalty state, and offers to defend them. Should they say yes? Should he take on the job? This is a truly hideous dilemma for them, and for him, and is thus a perfect subject for comedy.

Some dilemmas are hideous to the characters but trivial when viewed with an objective eye. The triviality will generally make them less funny, not more so. The important thing to understand is that the events of the comedy are deadly serious and potentially tragic *for the characters*. If they are not sufficiently important, the audience may feel that its time has been wasted.

6. The audience won't care if the characters don't.

A good comedy is not about silly people doing silly things. Comedy has to be about something important – important to the characters, and important to the society in which it is played. It is about serious characters doing desperate things because they have left themselves no choice.

Some critics, who should know better, have been known to use the word 'farce' pejoratively. When Antony Jay and I wrote our stage play *Yes Prime Minister* last year, we were fortunate and mostly received excellent reviews; but some critics complained that the play 'descends into farce'. A comedy cannot 'descend' into farce. That's like saying that a drama descends into tragedy.[1] A comedy can descend into *bad* comedy, but:

7. When a comedy is sufficiently funny, it *ascends* into farce.

Farce dramatises chaos but it is not in itself chaotic. A good farce is a perfectly organised exercise in duplicity, lust or several of the other Deadly Sins, a play or film full of truth and insight into the human condition, observing coldly and analytically where a tragedy might have elicited sympathy. It is not stupid, although the characters may behave stupidly.

Two of our greatest playwrights in the twentieth century

---

1 Besides which, those critics had clearly forgotten all the farcical scenes in the original series.

reached their greatest heights with farce. Joe Orton was one, and *Loot* is his masterpiece. Michael Frayn had previously enjoyed great success as a columnist, a novelist, a philosopher and a serious dramatic playwright, but in my opinion his greatest achievement came when he eventually wrote a farce, *Noises Off*.

In a good farce, the characters share the values of the society in which it is played. It is usually about serious people doing – and trying to cover up – desperate things that would be horribly embarrassing if they were discovered. They do them because their demons drive them, and they try to cover them up in order to maintain their dignity. Thus the logic of their actions, and their lies, forces them to behave in what appears to be a ridiculous way. For instance: a man comes out of a sleazy hotel bedroom with his neighbour's wife, sees the neighbour coming upstairs, races back into the bedroom, and hides in the fireplace with his head up a chimney full of soot, while the wife jams her husband's hat down over his eyes so that he can't recognise her. This is only funny *if they have no other choice*.[2]

Today the purpose of drama is mainly entertainment. But plays and films continue to show people what *not* to do. They show people breaking the rules and suffering the consequences. Drama was originally, anthropologically, a training programme for survival. And it still is.

Eight years before that meeting with Peter Hall I was directing *Anna Christie* at Stratford, and a friend of mine, Ron Eyre, was directing *Othello* in the RSC's main house. He was a fine director, but it was rumoured that the production was not going well. I saw him sitting alone in the bar one night

2   This happens in *A Little Hotel on the Side*.

after his fourth preview, having a quiet, solitary drink. 'How's *Othello* going?' I asked. 'Not bad,' he said. 'We've got nearly all the laughs out.'

In tragedy you have to get the laughs out, and in comedy you have to get the laughs in. It's the same process, however, merely inverted. Both involve sophisticated and craftsman-like control of the audience's response.

It was this conversation with Ron that gave me the idea for my proposal to Peter Hall, when I met him to discuss my programme for the Cottesloe: I wanted to direct an experimental production that would demonstrate how closely related tragedy and farce are to each other. I proposed a double production of *Macbeth*, a play that I know well and love: there would be two different views of it, playing alternate nights or alternate weeks, one as tragedy, one as farce. It would use the same set, the same costumes and all of the same actors save one – Macbeth would be different. Brian Cox, I hoped, would star in the tragic version and John Cleese in the funny one. I had phoned Cleese and he had already expressed interest in doing it. The essential point was that not one line would be changed.

I had previously directed *Macbeth* in a production with Brian and Gemma Jones. If I had to name a favourite play, that would be it: perhaps the most profound dramatic account of guilt ever written, three hundred years before Freud. But like all tragedies, it is desperately funny if you look at it through different eyes: three crazed witches chanting nonsense around a cauldron, the greedily ambitious Lady Macbeth, the foolishly trusting King Duncan, ghosts appearing and vanishing at dinner and all over the place, funny fights in chain mail, gallons of stage blood everywhere and lines like 'What? You egg!' The comic possibilities are endless, as everyone who has ever directed it knows – and fears. It even has a few 'Knock knock/Who's there?' jokes in the infamous porter scene, which is believed by many people to be there as comic relief and which in fact is extremely and, in my view, purposely unfunny. Anyone who saw the calamitous *Macbeth* with O'Toole years ago can testify to how side-splitting the play can be. The Old Vic was rocking with laughter.

I explained my *Macbeth* idea to Peter Hall. Peter stared at me for about a minute, in complete silence. Then he simply changed the subject and never referred to the idea again.

I think he pitied me.

I still want to try it, one day.

* * *

8. Comedy is like Time. *A* comedy is like *the* time.

We all know what *the* time is if we look at a clock, but no one knows what Time is. There is the same difference between 'comedy' and '*a* comedy'.

'*A* comedy' could be defined variously as something that makes us laugh, or has a happy ending, or is funny. Dictionary definitions of comedy are:

1. a play, movie, etc., of light and humorous character with a happy or cheerful ending; a dramatic work in which the central motif is the triumph over adverse circumstance, resulting in a successful or happy conclusion.
2. that branch of the drama which concerns itself with this form of composition.
3. the comic element of drama, of literature generally, or of life.

4. any literary composition dealing with a theme suitable for comedy, or employing the methods of comedy.
5. any comic or humorous incident or series of incidents.

Apart from the happy ending, which may or may not be a necessary part of the definition, these definitions all beg the question. Comedy is something that is comic, they say. Not much help. Maybe we can agree that comedy is what makes us laugh. Or tries to, anyway.

So, to put the question another way: what is funny? That's not much easier to answer. We all have our own views about that, often very different from each other. 'Funny' is a matter of opinion and of taste. But that won't do as a definition. My rule is to follow Carl Reiner's definition, the only workable definition of 'funny' that I have ever heard:

9. If you put it up there on the screen and they laugh, it's funny. If they don't laugh, it's not funny.

This is an objective test. You can't fake funniness.

This rule applies as much to the stage as the screen, of course. However, it presupposes (a) a full house and (b) a cross-section of the target audience. To achieve that you probably need at least two hundred people. More than two hundred would be better. Many more would be much better. If I go to a play or film and everyone in the audience laughs but me, I don't say it's not funny, I say that I didn't find it funny.

If you are writing or directing a comedy film, the test-screening process, so hated and derided by many film-makers, is vital because – unfortunately – nobody knows what is funny until we have seen and heard the audience's reaction.

We may think we know, and with enough experience we may often or even usually know, but there can be no certainty until it has been played in front of an audience. So to understand 'funny', or comedy, you have to examine the audience's response.

This is not new, nor is the process confined to film. Many film directors, who tend to have a vividly romantic view of themselves as artists, seem unwilling to do what theatre directors have always done and know is necessary: try it out. New comedies for the theatre have always opened outside London or New York, in a regional theatre or 'on the road', whether in Leeds, Brighton or Richmond, or Philadelphia, Boston or New Haven. The audience will tell us if we are going wrong.

Group behaviour changes people. It usually reduces their inhibitions and frequently makes them react with less empathy and more cruelty. We see this tribal or group behaviour in football crowds, gangs, armies, politically inspired mobs . . . and audiences.

10. An audience is more than a collection of individuals.

An audience is a thing unto itself, a specific type of crowd. Crowd psychology is different from individual psychology. This particular crowd needs to be made into a single and co-operative unit. That's why most people start a speech with a couple of jokes: they are organising a bunch of one hundred, five hundred or one thousand separate individuals into one group, one audience. That's why comedy works better in a full house than an empty one, why it's funnier to see a funny movie in a full theatre than at home on video: laughter is, from an evolutionary standpoint, a group activity. There is safety in numbers. It heightens the effect if we all react to-gether.

Antony Jay, my friend and writing partner on *Yes Minister* and *Yes Prime Minister*, remarks that when we laugh, 'We bare our teeth and emit a barking sound.'[3] In every other species such behaviour is immediately recognised as a warning or as aggression.

11. Laughter is aggressive behaviour.

Although we associate laughter with warm, happy experiences, it is the exact opposite if you're on the receiving end. It is when you are laughed *at* that you feel the aggression.

Many great comedies, and tragedies, revolve around being cruelly laughed at: Malvolio's scenes in *Twelfth Night* on the one hand, and the first two acts of *Rigoletto* on the other. And that cruelty is why comedians regard audiences as a dangerous beast that has to be subdued and ultimately killed.

12. The hope is to 'knock 'em dead!'

When I was directing *Loot* in 1984, John Lahr told me his theory that comedy is a matter of life and death for comics. He knew. His father Bert was a comedian, and he understood this from his earliest days. If their act goes well comedians say, 'I killed them,' 'I slayed them.' If the show has gone badly the comedian says, 'I died.' That represents, accurately, how they feel.

The comedian, and the comedy, is in a fight to the death

---

3   In a lecture, 'Understanding Laughter', which was delivered at the Royal Institution on 11 May 1990 and is published in *The Proceedings of the Royal Institution*, Vol. 62, 1990. Published by Science Reviews Ltd.

with the audience. A draw is not a satisfactory outcome for either side.

13. All comedy professionals fear the audience.

Some writers and directors are too scared to attend the first preview or the press night of their show. Many have to be fortified with stiff drinks. Most actors, but *all* comedy actors, suffer from stage fright. This includes the greatest talents, who perhaps suffer even more than most.

Robin Williams was quoted in the *New York Times*, talking about the problem of dealing with audiences: 'I guess it's that fear that they'll recognize – as you know – how insecure are we really? How desperately insecure that made us do *this* for a living.'

In 1975 Amnesty International asked John Cleese to put on a charity show. The idea was to gather together all the famous Oxbridge comedians on one stage for three nights. All the Pythons agreed to do it, except Eric Idle. So did the cast of *Beyond the Fringe* – Peter Cook, Alan Bennett and Jonathan Miller, and it was hoped Dudley Moore might even come over from Hollywood (he didn't). John Bird, John Fortune and Eleanor Bron were willing to help, and The Goodies too. Barry Humphries had promised to join in. John Cleese wanted to know if I would direct it.

I had directed several plays but I felt unable to handle a stage full of these icons, all of whom seemed so brilliant and confident. I admired – no, idolised – the cast of *Beyond the Fringe*. My generation of comedians sometimes fell back on sheer silliness, and frequently lacked the coruscating wit of Alan Bennett and Peter Cook. The idea of directing them or Jonathan Miller was terrifying and inconceivable.

Had I known just how unconfident, needy and depressed most of these icons were, I might have given a different answer. Instead, as it was such a good cause, I offered to help in any other way at all, whereupon John asked me to act in a sketch with him. It was called 'The Last Supper'. He had written it for *Monty Python* but the BBC had banned it, calling it blasphemous. He wanted to try it out.

John got Jonathan Miller to stage the show. Miller wasn't a bit nervous. Called *A Poke in the Eye*, it was to be performed at Her Majesty's Theatre for three successive nights at the beginning of April 1976. It was sold out within a few hours of the tickets going on sale, and a fourth night was added. The whole thing was to be filmed by a documentary filmmaker, Roger Graef, not just the performances but also the preparation and rehearsals.[4] This process was revealing about the participants: some, like Jonathan Miller and Peter Cook, came alive in rehearsal whenever the lights and the camera turned towards them, sparkling and thrusting themselves wittily forward. Others (Eleanor Bron and I, for instance) froze and can occasionally be glimpsed edging furtively backwards out of the door when the camera pointed in our direction.

'The Last Supper' was typical of John at his best: an argument between the Pope and Michelangelo about a painting that the Pope (Cleese) had commissioned but didn't care

---

4   Roger Graef's film of those nights came out under the title *Pleasure at Her Majesty's*. It was the first in what eventually became a series of annual performances, although the next show, *The Secret Policeman's Ball*, didn't happen until three years later. Then came *The Secret Policeman's Other Ball*, establishing a tradition that led to Live Aid and Comic Relief. Fortunes were raised for a variety of good causes, but there was a charm and an innocence about that first show, a bunch of well-intentioned, funny people unselfishly getting together in support of a charity that stood for human rights and freedom of speech, to make a statement against political imprisonment and torture.

for because it featured twenty-nine disciples, a couple of kangaroos and three Christs.[5] Michelangelo felt that the Pope's demands were an unwarranted and petty attack on his artistic vision and freedom of expression.

Although all the participants in the show were on their best and most gentlemanly behaviour, there is an undeniable air of competition when twenty comedians gather together, even for Amnesty International, and the level of anxiety is sky-high. Rita, my wife, inadvertently wounded Alan Bennett that night, when she passed him on the stairs backstage and told him how much she had enjoyed his NORWICH ('Nickers Off Ready When I Come Home') sketch. The following evening, just before the second performance, I heard that Jonathan Miller was looking everywhere for me. I went to find him. 'What did Rita say to Alan last night?' he asked, his eyebrows almost perpendicular with anxiety.

'She said she loved NORWICH.'

'Alan did two monologues last night. Didn't she mention the other one?'

'I don't know.'

'Oh God! I don't think she did. And nobody else said they liked it either. He doesn't want to go on tonight. Please find Rita and see if she can help.'

I found her. She found Alan. He was sitting alone and depressed in an empty chorus dressing room six floors up. She told him that she loved both sketches. Alan brightened a little, went on that night and was brilliantly funny as usual. Rita was relieved. I never forgot this tiny incident because it was so strange. I didn't know Alan well, and he hardly knew Rita at all. Why did it matter to him what Rita thought?

---

5   You can find it on YouTube.

It mattered because he thought he'd died.

A few days after *A Poke in the Eye* John called and asked if I could get Alan to agree to be in it the following year. I phoned him. 'Alan,' I said, 'Amnesty made so much money that they want us all to do it again next year.'

'Oh *no!*' he moaned. 'That's like saying "Let's have *another* crucifixion next Friday."'

14. Audience aggression must be harnessed so that the show is in control of it.

In all comedy, the performers, actors and director (if there is one) must get the audience on their side.

15. The audience laughs because it recognises something truthful.

Tom Stoppard, I read, called laughter the sound of comprehension. I have always thought of it as the sound of recognition. We laugh when we see something on the stage or screen that rings true: there, but for the grace of God, go I!

With their laughter, everyone in the group is agreeing to accept the truth you are telling. There are certain exceptions that I'll come to: we don't laugh if what we are watching doesn't ring true, or if it seems false or silly.

So what do we do? We do what in any other species would be rightly seen as aggressive behaviour. We bark with recognition, like dogs do when their owner comes home.

If in a play or a film we don't recognise some truth about ourselves, or someone we know, if it has been heightened or exaggerated too much for the situation, we don't find the comedy funny. We say it's silly or stupid.

Easy recognition of human behaviour is why so many silent film comedies – those of Chaplin, Keaton, Harold Lloyd, Laurel and Hardy – played successfully in every culture, whereas many dialogue-driven comedies don't travel.[6] Frequently this is because of local references: an American audience may laugh if you make a joke about Kmart or Walmart, but in the rest of the world they won't know what you're talking about. There is no recognition.

If you make a baseball comedy, it will not play in most countries outside the US. If you make a film about football – soccer, as they call it in America – it is most unlikely to be a blockbuster because most Americans still don't play it. No recognition.

Language is also a problem: if you make a film in the UK and refer to a decision as 'swings and roundabouts', it will not be understood in the US. In the US you would say 'It's a wash', which the Brits wouldn't understand. I have an English/American dictionary, in which over four thousand words have different meanings in our two countries. Jokes have to be instantly recognisable and understood. In a film, it helps to get laughs if you use dialogue that means the same thing in every English-speaking country, or else the context has to be so clear that the meaning can be easily and instantly inferred.

---

6 Shooting silent film is always called m.o.s. for short. This dates from the 1930s and 1940s, when there were so many refugee directors in Hollywood from Germany, Austria, Hungary and Czechoslovakia who said 'mit-out sound'. The other, nearly forgotten term from the same period is v.a.v., which you said if you wanted to clear the set for shooting: it stood for 'valk away'. At one point, in fact, there were so many central European directors in Hollywood that a sign was posted in the Paramount Commissary: 'To be Hungarian is not enough.'

16. If we laugh because we recognise something *about ourselves*, we are owning up.

Frequently when we laugh we are admitting: I've said that, I've done that, I've thought that or *I wish* I'd said that or done that.

Or, more aggressively: *You* have done that, or said that, and that's why I'm laughing at you. You might be subconsciously adding: I dislike you, I despise you, I am contemptuous of your behaviour.

You will laugh more if you are surrounded by other people who are laughing because they share your view. They're owning up too.

17. Audiences are more likely to own up if they are in the dark.

Apart from the obvious reason that lights focus their attention, the audience laughs more if they are in the dark because they are not owning up in public. Being in the dark takes the potential embarrassment out of it for the audience.

18. Before the audience is admitted, the temperature in the theatre should not be more than 65 degrees Fahrenheit.

Or maybe 68 degrees if it's really well, and silently, air-conditioned. People do not laugh when they get hot. They smile. You want them to laugh! A big theatre that is at 65 degrees when the doors open will heat up a lot with hundreds of people in it. You want it cool – not cold, but cool.

19. Empty seats are a big deterrent to laughter.

The house must be full, especially if it has fewer than two hundred seats. This is particularly important for press nights, test screenings and premieres. Empty seats are as big a threat to laughter as an overheated theatre.

20. The audience must be new to the show. They must not have seen it before.

Many a press night in the West End or on Broadway, and many a film premiere, has been spoiled because the audience is made up of people who have seen it before and want it to succeed *too much*.

These people include: producers, investors, production staff, agents, managers and the spouses of anyone involved in the production. If they come to previews, they should not be seated on the opening night.

Nobody laughs at a comedy as much as when they see it for the first time. The second, third, fourth or umpteenth time contains no surprises. Furthermore, all of the aforementioned producers, investors, production staff, agents, managers and spouses will be much too anxious to laugh anyway. Rabbit's friends and relations make a bad audience on an important occasion.

21. People with an axe to grind should not come to press nights.

This group includes:

people who can't see why they weren't cast in it;

people who can't see why this play or film should succeed when theirs didn't;

people who have a show of their own opening in the next few weeks and think that there isn't room for two hit comedies (there always is);

people who think that they are experts on the subject (for instance, politicians at *Yes Prime Minister* or historians at historical plays), because they may want to demonstrate their expertise by disparaging what they see.

You need a fresh reaction: this means that, apart from the press, the audience should be *the general public*.

* * *

My first real professional job in a comedy was at the Belgrade Theatre in Coventry.

'I know you!' Robert Chetwyn, the artistic director, greeted me when I walked in to audition. He was a bluff, be-spectacled man with a loud, nervous laugh. 'I saw you in the Cambridge Footlights revue.' I had graduated a few months before.

For his spring season he wanted a company of young character actors. Would I agree to play 'as cast'? I would have agreed to anything. I wanted to learn my craft in rep. I saw myself as a character actor, certainly capable of playing comedy, but with my sights set on more 'important' work. Who knows what I meant by that? I fancied that I was a young Alec Guinness or Charles Laughton. I didn't tell Chetwyn that, of course. Two days later I was phoned and told that he wanted me to start the following Monday in Coventry at twelve pounds a week.

It all seemed so romantic. My first theatrical digs. The landlady, Mrs Kohler, gave me a clean attic room with bed and breakfast for three pounds ten shillings a week, or four pounds if I wanted heating. She was big, round and blonde, with a wet cough, a Czech accent and a cynical sense of humour. She told me proudly that she'd once had Stephen Boyd, one of the stars of *Ben-Hur*. I presumed she meant as a lodger.

The comedy was *The Taming of the Shrew*, which was directed not by Chetwyn but by a character actor who occasionally directed in rep. He was a burly, genial man, utterly obsessed with sex. He was always touching the women in the company, putting his hands on their knees and telling unfunny sexist jokes. I was playing Grumio, and I was disheartened to find out that not only was the director no help, he was actually an enemy of comedy. At one point he told me to run up a ladder into a barn loft, say a couple of lines, then jump down. When I asked why, he said that I was playing a clown and such questions didn't apply: clowns can do anything and I should just accept that anything is possible within the 'clown convention'.

22. Clowns are not intrinsically funny.

The same rules of comedy apply to clowns as to everyone else. Marcel Marceau was not funny. Circus clowns are hardly ever funny.

And I wasn't playing a clown, I was playing Petruchio's servant.

23. Avoid unmotivated 'comic business'.

Much 'comic business' was imposed on the cast at the very first rehearsal, most of which was unfunny and unmotivated. The worst and most embarrassing was that Petruchio was to tip a full bucket of custard over my head in the scene when he brings Katherine to his house. I tried to explain to the director that it would never get a laugh as two other servants had had several buckets of water tipped over them shortly before I entered. The joke, if there was one, was over.

The director was impervious. All he ever said to me was, 'Don't think so much.' So, for the run of that show, every night for nearly three weeks, Petruchio poured a sweetened yellow avalanche over my head while nine hundred people in the audience watched quietly. Not once did it get a laugh. There was actually no sound at all, not even heavy breathing. I exited, slowly, blindly, dripping sticky custard, in the embarrassing silence that followed.

This 'comic business' dismally failed the Carl Reiner test (Rule 9). We put it up there in front of no less than nine hundred people and nobody laughed. Hence, no matter what the director said, it was not funny. It also failed the recognition test and the owning-up test: as nobody laughed, it indicated that no one saw any truth in it. They were right. There was no truth in it. There was nothing to own up to.

You don't get over this sort of humiliation fast, especially when you're twenty-one, but over the three-week run of *The Shrew* the sense of shame slowly lessened. It became clear that the more experienced members of the cast felt as screwed up by the director as I did. New actors joined the company and they said they hated the show but liked me in it; I'm sure it wasn't true, but actors often lie to each other because

24. You can't be funny if you lose your nerve.

The audience needs to feel they are in safe hands. Stand-up acts in which the basic joke is lack of confidence (Woody Allen or Tommy Cooper) paradoxically need to be performed confidently.

The lies of my fellow actors helped me. I was grateful for these straws and I clutched onto them.

25. Romantic comedy requires a good reason why the man and the woman cannot be together.

The Shrew is often thought of as a romantic comedy. Like *Much Ado About Nothing*, the resistance that keeps the leading characters from seeing that they were meant for each other comes from the fact that they are so alike. Other external elements can help romantic comedy: class differences, for instance, are instant shorthand for why two characters in a romantic comedy should not get along (*It Happened One Night*).

Romantic comedy is about what happens when two people who are in love, or might be, are kept apart by character differences, parental disapproval, class, economic, cultural or ethnic differences. Today there are so few taboos in Western democracies that it is increasingly hard to make such obstacles and impediments credible, and devices have become somewhat contrived. The successful film *Sleepless in Seattle* came up with a unique solution, preventing the two protagonists from meeting at all until the final shot of the film.

If two people desperately want to get together because they're in love, whether or not they know it, you have the basis of romantic comedy from Shakespeare to the present day. But if they just want to get together for sex, not love, that would not be a romantic comedy: that would be a farce, or what Hollywood calls a broad comedy. This is because sex and lust, when viewed objectively, are intrinsically ludicrous.

The Shrew played in repertory with Jean Anouilh's *Becket*. I was cast as the Pope, Third Baron and the Archbishop of York, so most of my time during the performances was spent running upstairs to the dressing room and down again, changing costumes. Everybody in the play except Becket, the King, the French Princess and the four Barons wore masks. At the slow, dull dress rehearsal Chetwyn jumped up on the stage and said with great frustration: '*Come on* everybody! Nobody's reacting to what's going on here between Thomas and the King.' He turned to me. 'Jonathan, react! You're supposed to be getting all lathered up.'

I was playing the Archbishop of York in the scene, and reacting was a bit of a problem because no part of my body was actually visible: I wore a mask on my face, a mitre on my head, robes down to the floor, gloves on my hands, and all my lines had been cut. How could I react, I wondered? When they started the scene again and a big reaction seemed called for, I fell over.

26. Masks don't help comedy.

They obscure all reactions, except the very largest ones.

27. Beware the costume that makes the audience laugh when they're not supposed to.

I didn't have to wear a mask as the Third Baron but my chain mail was knitted out of string, sprayed with grey paint, and it kept expanding. The leggings were so heavy that gravity caused them to roll down into large folds around my ankles and legs, so that I looked like the Michelin Man. The only solution seemed to be to tie them higher around my waist but, due to their weight, the trousers still kept drooping. I tied them higher and higher until finally, three weeks into the run, they were fastened around my neck. It was just as well the run ended then, or I'd have had to pull them right up through the neck of my tunic, under the helmet, secure them over the top of my head, and cut a hole in the flies for my face.

28. You have a problem if your costume makes the audience cry.

That Christmas I played Mikey the Baby Dragon in *Beauty and the Beast*. I was supposed to be the lovable comedy person. Unfortunately, an enthusiastic young costume designer had decreed that I should wear a really heavy, blue and silver fibreglass dragon costume. It had huge, fearsome spikes all the way down the back, and a helmet that forced me to stand like a marsupial with scoliosis and which hid most of my face. At the rear end of the spikes was a long clanking tail. The designer was deeply proud of her creation, but when I bounced lovably onto the stage at the first performance all the kids cried.

There were other problems. Once in it, I could neither stand up straight nor sit down, and had to spend the next hour and a half in a sort of crouching fisticuffs pose. I complained, to no avail. On the third performance, crouching wallaby-like in the wings, exhausted from the weight of the spike-suit, I dropped to my knees and then flopped forward onto my tummy. At last I'd found a way to relax in my costume. When I heard my cue approaching, I tried to stand up – and found that I couldn't. I was trapped like a knight in medieval armour, lying face downwards on the stage floor.

Unfortunately the stage manager didn't know I was there. She was on the other side of the stage. I heard her voice whispering urgently over the tannoy: 'Mr Lynn on stage please. Mr Lynn, on stage please!' I flapped around on the floor like a fish out of water, calling 'Help!' and 'I'm here!' in a stentorian whisper. Nobody heard. My cue arrived. 'Calling Mr Lynn. Mr Lynn on stage *now* please!' The actors on stage, having run out of dialogue, started some feeble ad-libbing. The kids in the audience were sounding restless. I could hear assistant stage managers running all over the theatre, looking for me, calling my name in the corridor, knocking on dressing-room doors. Finally one of them thought of looking in the wings. She tried to pick me up but it was impossible – nothing short of a crane or the entire stage-management team would be able to hoist me. Raised to my feet at last, I clanked badtemperedly onto the stage only to be met once more by the crying of numerous terrified kids.

I said I wasn't going on again until I had a costume I could work in. This caused consternation and there were mutterings about 'difficult actors' in the wardrobe department. Then, incredibly, somebody found that a company in London called Theatre Zoo had an available, ready-to-wear dragon's costume. I was promised that it contained no fibreglass. When it arrived it didn't look anything at all like a dragon, more like a large green Babygro with a tail and ears, but it was better than the other. I put it on, pronounced it workable, and the costume designer burst into floods of tears and fled. I went on that afternoon and not one of the kids cried. A low ambition achieved!

The season at Coventry finished with a week of *The Cocktail Party* by T. S. Eliot: I was a Caterer's Man, a walk-on, but it meant twelve extra quid. Rowland Davies and I livened up this dull, pretentious play with an inventive, slapstick turn as the two Caterer's Men, much to the disapproval of the cast and the delight of the audience, who gave us a big round of applause on our exit every night. We probably should have been fired. Why was it funny? Because of the recognisable truth in our clumsiness, something rather lacking in the rest of the evening.

29. 'Ridiculous' and 'absurd' are not synonyms for 'funny'.

Absurdist theatre tends to be treated with respect. Ridiculous theatre does not. The difference between them tends to be a matter of opinion. 'Absurd' theatre is highly regarded by critics and by people who are under the mistaken impression that the equation *absurd = funny* is true.[7]

The Shrew remains the only time that I have acted in Shakespeare, which used to sadden me. It doesn't any more. There was one other occasion when it nearly happened: the experimental director Charles Marowitz asked me to play Hamlet. 'I see Hamlet as a kind of a buffoon, which is why you were my first choice,' said Marowitz when we met.

I sipped the gritty cup of Nescafé that he had provided but hadn't stirred very well. 'Thank you,' I said.

---

7   It's true in a good production of *Waiting for Godot*. Rarely otherwise. Few playwrights can sustain it well for a full evening.

Marowitz was a big American, maybe a New Yorker, with a black beard, a shiny, patent-leather comb-over and a wide, confident smile. 'This is gonna be different from the usual *Hamlet*. I'm restructuring it, rethinking it, to get the essence. There's a lotta teaching in the play so I'm setting it in a classroom. Gertrude is gonna be the teacher because, ya know, she's the kinda mother-figure.' (Not so much the mother-figure as the mother, I thought.) 'The problem with the play is that there's a *lotta* clichés in it. You know, "To be or not to be", "To thine own self be true" and shit like that, and Polonius says a lot of it, so everyone's gonna sit around in a circle and whenever anybody says a cliché the rest of the cast is gonna laugh and applaud, ironically.'

I racked my brains but I couldn't think of anything appropriate to say.

'Would you like to read the script?' he asked. I nodded. He gave it to me and ushered me into the room next door. It seemed that it was a confidential document and I wasn't allowed to leave with it. It was also very short. It was odd to find lines in it from *Othello*, and I was startled to read, 'Enter Rosencrantz and Guildenstern, dressed as a vaudeville song and dance team, tied together with a rope, clutching their balls.' In retrospect I can see a point of view in that instruction but, disappointed not to be offered Hamlet as I knew it, I declined the part. That was in about 1966, and I was never again offered a role in Shakespeare. I'm happy that I have directed his plays once or twice over the years.

The critics found his *Hamlet* 'interesting'. Marowitz was a drama critic too, a colleague of theirs, and the play, now called *The Marowitz Hamlet*, was really a critic's view of Hamlet's madness. The original interested me more. Also, I didn't want to be laughed *at*, only *with*. I preferred to get laughs that I intended to get and thus stay in control of that dangerous beast, the audience.

30. Although you must control them, the audience is your friend, not your enemy.

The audience is like a dog because, not only does it bark and bare its teeth, it can be easily trained to love you: it wants leadership. Audiences enjoy being part of the pack. The audience gains confidence when the performers are confident, it wants the performers to be in control, it likes a safe pair of hands. The audience reacts badly to poor leadership, lack of control and failure to set boundaries.

Members of the audience have made a commitment. They could be watching TV, playing video games, chess or whatever they would do if they stayed at home. They have not gone to a pub, a restaurant, a football game or any other entertainment. They have come to see you, your show. And, usually, they have paid to see it. That is a serious investment of time and money.

This means that, like Alfred P. Doolittle in *Pygmalion*, the audience is wanting to like you, it's willing to like you, it's waiting to like you. On the other hand, it needs you to be confident, in charge and to know what you are doing. Then it will relax and be happy.

None of this applies, however, to people who have been given free seats. These seats are called 'paper'. If the theatre is full of people who have not paid, the house is said to be 'papered'. This will be a tough crowd. They have made no commitment. They may think – or know – that they are doing you a favour by being there. They know that demand to see the show is low or they wouldn't have been given the comps. They have low expectations. Many, like the critics, are there not because they want to be but because they have to be. This kind of audience will never react as well as a house full of paying customers, but even they can be won round.

31. There are days when the audience will always be difficult:

New Year's Eve
Heatwaves, with no air conditioning
Snowstorms, with icy roads and uncertain trains
Hurricanes
Terrorist attacks
Death of Princess Diana
Royal Weddings
Royal Funerals
Declaration of War days, especially futile wars that the public doesn't believe in
And any other day when it is hard for any normal person to relax and enjoy themselves.

The more determined an audience is to enjoy itself, the better. Monday nights can be wonderful. Saturday nights, though generally the fullest houses, are not usually the best. Saturday audiences tend to be people who just wanted to go out somewhere because it's Saturday night; Monday night audiences tend to be people who specifically want to see your show.

* * *

I hoped to become an actor when I left Cambridge, but under pressure from my parents to have 'something to fall back on' I was studying law, mainly because it seemed the right preparation for politics, the other 'respectable' career that attracted me. Why people consider politicians respectable was unclear to me then, and still is. Lawyering, unfortunately, is a lifelong habit, and hard to break; I still regard myself as a recovering lawyer.

I had grown up in a household where politics were discussed all day, every day. An uncle of mine had been Secretary of the Cambridge Union Society, a glorified debating society, when he was up at Cambridge (it was assumed that you went 'up' to Oxford or Cambridge and 'down' to anywhere else), and my parents had given me a lifetime subscription to the Union in the vain hope that I might even exceed my uncle's achievement and become President.

It was the richest club in Cambridge, with a grand Victorian building and an impressive debating chamber like a mini-House of Commons. Members could listen to debates on the floor of the chamber, sitting behind the principal speakers for whichever side of the motion they supported, and they could speak briefly if called upon. Guests and women, in that order of importance, sat in the gallery. Like Westminster, it was posturing political theatre that decides nothing and achieves less. Famous guest speakers came but were always preceded by four undergraduates, two for and two against the motion. The undergraduate speakers, the President and the Secretary all wore white tie and tails, and the style of the debate was formal and pompous, making a curious contrast with the youth of the speakers and the pimply puerility of much of what was being said.

The speakers included a number of ambitious and smug young men like Michael Howard and John Selwyn Gummer, who undoubtedly saw themselves as future members of a Tory government. Distressingly, less than twenty years later, that's who they were, and still wearing the same self-satisfied expressions as they sat on the front bench. I knew Michael a little, and John a little more. Like all politicians, they were charming and often thoroughly entertaining in private, but their unwarranted confidence in their own abilities was a sight to behold when they were twenty. It is odd that politicians think so highly of themselves, when all the evidence is that nobody else does.

32. Vanity, pomposity and hypocrisy are intrinsically funny.

I soon realised I could never be a politician, and that the most useful contribution I could make to society would be to ridicule them when necessary. Fortunately, in Britain, unlike many parts of the world, we have the luxury of being able to do that without being shot or put under house arrest. This could have happened to me had I lived in the wrong country, not because I'm brave, which I'm not, but because I'm reckless and opinionated and I find it terribly hard to keep my mouth shut.

All the university societies had open meetings for 'freshers'. The one at the Amateur Dramatic Club was discouraging. Incredibly confident undergraduate actors and directors introduced us to the ADC's own theatre, using lots of professional terminology like 'floats' and 'front tabs' (footlights and the front curtain, also known as 'the rag'). I had no idea what they were talking about. When I learned that the excellent production of *The Taming of the Shrew* that I had seen at the Arts Theatre in my first week was not professional, as I'd assumed, but directed by a third-year undergraduate called Trevor Nunn, I decided that I'd be way out of my depth and didn't even apply for membership.

Varsity was the university newspaper, run by students, and next I tried writing for it. I won a competition for the best freshman article (the competition must have been poor or non-existent) and was offered a 'job' as a reporter. The editor was the slightly stooping Benedict Nightingale, theatre critic of *The Times* until his retirement last year, who seemed like a world-weary denizen of Fleet Street even at the age of twenty. The news editor was a large, cheerful, feckless youth with big square glasses. His name was Peter Pagnamenta. If the paper was short of news he drummed up sensational stories: when the Ballet Rambert came to the Arts Theatre he phoned up the company manager and asked if it was true that their prima ballerina had landed so heavily in a *pas de deux* that she'd gone through the stage floor. Gleefully, he printed their denial as a story: BALLET RAMBERT DENIES BALLERINA WENT THROUGH STAGE FLOOR ON HEAVY LANDING, or words to that effect. Peter went on to become an editor, not of the *Sun* but of the BBC's highly respectable *Panorama*. I decided that purveying half-truths in print was not one of my ambitions.

Instead I joined the University Jazz Band, a harmlessly pot-smoking and mildly delusional group. At one of the parties where we played a gig there was also a cabaret, a sophisticated word that I had always associated with Maurice Chevalier and topless Parisian showgirls. It turned out to mean a twenty-minute turn by two exceptionally tall young comedians. One was bearded, lantern-jawed and had piercing, round, staring eyes, and the other was blond and clumsy with big feet, sucking a pipe, whose awkward movement re-

33

minded me of Jacques Tati in *Monsieur Hulot's Holiday*. They were funny. I assumed they were professional comedians and wondered how and why they were there, but it turned out that one was a law student named John Cleese and the other a medic named Graham Chapman. They were members of the Footlights Club, which I had heard of because I'd seen *Beyond the Fringe* just before I went up to Cambridge and I'd read that Peter Cook, Jonathan Miller and David Frost had been members of it.

In my first year I had seen a number of ADC plays and discovered that all the confident talk at the freshers' meeting didn't actually amount to much. The acting was not that good and I needn't have been so humble. I decided to try my hand at acting and I was cast in Chekhov's *Ivanov*. Ivanov was played by a skinny Parsee future actor named Saam Dastoor, who slept on the floor of his rooms because a mattress was too comfortable. Too comfortable is a concept that I have yet to understand.

Also in my new circle of friends was Richard Eyre, a shy and introverted would-be actor who seemed to me to have little or no chance of success in his chosen profession. Stephen Frears (a law student like me, Cleese and Tim Brooke-Taylor) was also in *Ivanov*, and the following term he directed the old West End musical *Expresso Bongo*, written by Monty Norman and Julian More. Eyre played Bongo Herbert, the rock star, and seemed profoundly embarrassed by the experience.

Steve Frears was also curiously private; he had a shock of dark hair, a superior, brooding manner and a protruding, pouting lower lip. There were rumours that his family owned Frears Biscuits and that he was very rich, but I saw no sign of it. He was secretive and gave the impression that he was full of important thoughts. I played drums, led the band and was the musical director. I didn't have a clue what I was doing, but the production turned out fine and people enjoyed it.

Pembroke, my college, was known as the comedy college. Eric Idle, a lanky, skinny youth with a slight Midlands accent, a sweet smile and an endearing personality, buttonholed me about doing a sketch with him at the Pembroke smoker that spring. A 'smoker' was a sketch show, produced once a year by the Pembroke Players, accompanied by much drinking and all in black tie. This event had assumed minor importance in Cambridge because Peter Cook had recently been at Pembroke and now Tim Brooke-Taylor and Bill Oddie were there. Eric suggested to me that we write something funny together. I didn't know how, and said no. Eric was undaunted, and soon returned with a sketch about two guards on duty outside Buckingham Palace.

33. If you want to be a writer, start writing and keep writing.

I was impressed. About fifteen years ago I found the page with the sketch on it at the bottom of a drawer. I had it framed and gave it to Eric for his birthday, the first sketch he ever wrote.

Eric went to talk to Bill Oddie, a jazz enthusiast whom I had often seen lurking shyly in dark corners at the Jazz Club. I liked Bill instantly. Stocky, diminutive and, like Eric, a grammar-school boy from somewhere around Birmingham, he was extremely reserved even on stage, and had four interests in life: bird-watching, playing rugby, music and writing funny material. I couldn't see much point in the first two[8]

---

8   As he became a famous ornithologist and naturalist with his own TV series, apparently there *was* some point.

and didn't know how he did the fourth. Tim was unlike Bill in every way – effortlessly upper-middle class, blond, smooth and an amusing speechmaker. Eric, Bill and I, all natural outsiders, slowly became friends. My funny turn with Eric in his sketch was well received, and Bill encouraged us to do it at the next Footlights smoker.

The Footlights Dramatic Club is a 120-year-old Cambridge institution. Essentially a comedy club, many of its alumni over the years have become mainstays of British comedy.[9] The clubroom was above a fishmonger's, approached through Falcon Yard off Petty Cury, since demolished for a new shopping mall. Though the whiff of old fish wafting up through the windows was less than appealing on a hot day, it was the cool place to have lunch because the membership was so exclusive. The only way to join the Footlights Club in those days was to make the committee laugh at a smoker.

Women were excluded from Footlights membership, though not from lunch. For the first time, I realised how conservative comedians can be.

34. Comedy, I'm sorry to say, is not necessarily subversive. It can be reactionary.

I had naively assumed that comedy is created by satirists who are critical of the way things are; I now saw that comedy could equally be created by angry reactionaries who resent change. This came as a disappointment to me. Most of the would-be comedians in the Footlights were in the opposite

---

9   Jimmy Edwards, Peter Shaffer, Michael Frayn, Bamber Gascoigne, David Frost, Peter Cook, Jonathan Miller, John Cleese, Graham Chapman, Eric Idle, Rowan Atkinson, Griff Rhys Jones, Robert Buckman, Hugh Laurie, Stephen Fry, Emma Thompson, Sacha Baron Cohen, to mention just a few.

political corner from me and the jazzniks, who were all lefties.

There was a campaign to allow women to join the Footlights, which was opposed by numerous incipient funnymen on the grounds that 'women aren't funny' or 'can't we have *somewhere* to go to get away from women?' Both arguments were idiotic, the latter because twenty out of the twenty-three Cambridge colleges were all-male. And who, I wondered, would want to get away from women? I spent my entire waking life trying to work out how to get as close to them as possible.

Many of those opposed to women joining the club had been to boys' boarding schools and were deeply apprehensive about the opposite sex. This was understandable, as some of the women who wanted to join were pretty scary, including a short, stout, foul-mouthed, entertaining lesbian called Miriam Margolyes and a tall, gangling, foul-mouthed, entertaining Australian called Germaine Greer. I knew Miriam well and Germaine hardly at all, but I liked them both. They shook things up a bit. When Eric became President of the club in our last year, women were immediately invited to join.

35. It is hazardous to your career to make sexist jokes about women.

But you can make them about men. Straight men, of course, not gay men.

There are fashions in sexist jokes. In the sixties, many jokes were made by men about large boobs, knockers, tits, hooters and other euphemisms. Today it is considered bad taste to make a joke about big breasts, or any other kind of breast.

37

This has been one of the great successes of the women's movement. Curiously, those jokes have now been replaced by jokes about small penises. These jokes *are* acceptable, and indeed appear to be almost mandatory for male comedians to demonstrate how enlightened they are. These jokes can, of course, be made by both men and women.

My own personal rule is: Avoid breasts and penises, unless the joke is original and funny. Which is rare indeed. And remember:

36. There is no such thing as bad taste.

Something is funny, or it's not funny. When comedy is funny, it tells a truth that might otherwise not be told. 'Bad taste' is simply a way of describing when a joke has crossed the line into 'not funny'.

LA's Hillcrest Country Club was founded in 1920 by a group of Jews who worked in films but were not allowed to join the LA Country Club. (They still wouldn't be allowed to join, by the way.) It is the club about which Groucho Marx famously remarked, 'I would not join a club that would have me as a member,' although he did join, presumably because it was the only one he *could* join. It is said that Groucho was offered membership at one of the other golf clubs in LA, as long as he didn't use the swimming pool, and he replied, 'My daughter's only half Jewish, can she wade in up to her knees?'

All the moguls belonged to Hillcrest: Adolph Zukor of Paramount, Harry Cohn of Columbia, and the Warner Brothers. Much important movie history took place there: Louis B. Mayer punched Sam Goldwyn in the showers, presumably leading to the break-up of Metro-Goldwyn-Mayer. When the club eventually decided to open up membership to non-Jews, their first choice for a new member was comedian Danny Thomas (a Lebanese Catholic). One member remarked: 'If we're going to let in a gentile, can't we at least pick one who *looks* like a gentile?'

I was taken to brunch at Hillcrest by Ben Landis, an elderly and entertaining uncle of the director John Landis, an original member of Hillcrest and a judge on the California Superior Court.[10] He showed me the famous buffet. It was gigantic and loaded with fatty, high-calorie, delicious food: tons of cream and sour cream, eggs, red meats, breads, cheeses, ice creams of every flavour, everything you would want to eat that your cardiologist would advise against. 'How do you like the buffet?' Judge Landis asked me. 'They say it has killed more Jews than Hitler!'

I laughed. I found that funny, not offensive. I think it was because the joke was about the food, or maybe about Hitler. Although it related to the Holocaust, it did not directly refer to it. However, a joke that went around – 'Imelda Marcos had more women's shoes than Dachau' – is not funny. It's horrible, because it immediately conjures up in the mind's eye an image of a huge pile of shoes taken from corpses, and that then summons the image of the corpses themselves.

Are both jokes 'in bad taste'? Who cares? I don't. All comedy is in bad taste for somebody. The question is: Is it funny?

37. Jews can make Jewish jokes, gays can make gay jokes,

---

10 When the LA District Attorney brought obscenity charges against Lenny Bruce, he refused a Public Defender and insisted on representing himself. Ben Landis asked him what his defence would be, and Bruce replied that he would do his act in court. Ben allowed it, and then dismissed the charges. After that Bruce was prosecuted in San Francisco and lost that case.

the disabled can make disabled jokes, blacks can say 'nigger' . . . and so on.

This privilege is slight compensation for all the concomitant indignities. It is dangerous for others to make these jokes. Anyone, however, is allowed to make jokes about anyone who is not perceived as a member of a minority or victim group. And one last thing:

38. Everybody in the US has a moral duty to make jokes about Republicans.

* * *

Right after my second-year law exams was the annual Footlights Revue at the Arts Theatre. It was called *A Clump of Plinths*, and it was the revue which launched the careers of John Cleese, Graham Chapman, Bill Oddie, Tim Brooke-Taylor, David Hatch[11] and Jo Kendall. Not me. I played the drums, in the orchestra pit. It was there that I came across my first rule of comedy – not the most important, but the first I learned:

39. If the band – or the film crew – laugh loudly at a joke, you should probably cut it.

The band will only laugh at any new line which is a variation of the original. This is because they are so bored. But usually, to find the variation funny, you have to know what was there before. It is what vaudeville comedians used to call 'bananas

---

11 Eventually, Managing Director of BBC Radio.

on bananas'. A joke on a joke. Hilarious to insiders, baffling to everyone else.

Most comedians take years of trial and error to find their own comic style, but Cleese burst onto the Arts Theatre stage with his unique persona of British inhibition and repressed rage fully realised. Coupled with his characteristic bizarre and insane movement, his comedy has remained essentially unchanged ever since, though of course it gained dimension and depth eleven years later when he wrote the first *Fawlty Towers* series with his wife Connie Booth, and the second series four years after that with his ex-wife Connie Booth. Some of his performances in that 1963 Footlights revue show – the uptight colonial married couple John and Mary on a humid Far Eastern porch (later it became a staple of *I'm Sorry, I'll Read That Again*), his MI5 spymaster interviewing a candidate, his 'BBC BC' biblical weather report forecasting the Ten Plagues ('And moving in from the South-South-West: boils!') – were as funny as anything he's ever done.

A Clump of Plinths got sensational reviews in a couple of national newspapers and attracted the attention of Michael White, a well-heeled, drawling, twenty-seven-year-old producer with lazy charm, a man so laid back as to be virtually horizontal. He was a gambler. He loved poker. His father broke the bank at Cannes and he was brought up in great splendour in Switzerland. Like Sky Masterson in *Guys and Dolls*, he would have bet on which raindrop would get to the bottom of the window first. He had already produced three or four minor but interesting West End shows, most recently *The Connection*, a controversial play with jazz about drug addiction, and he offered to take the Footlights into the West End. The title was changed to *Cambridge Circus*.

It opened in the West End to mixed reviews, but more good than bad. All the critics proclaimed Bill Oddie the star of the show, which irritated Cleese. It was because of John and Bill, two exceedingly angry people at that time – John's rage was repressed and Bill's was right out there – that I began to get some insight into one of the basic facts about comedians and comedy writers:

40. All comedians and comedy writers are angry.

They may not realise it. They may be in denial. They may repress their anger or they may release its full destructive power. They may not show it if they're getting older, have had therapy or simply mellowed with age or success. But they are or were angry: I have met hundreds, worked closely with many and lived with myself. In my experience it's invariable.

It is pretty well agreed among psychologists and psycho-therapists of all stripes that everybody has, deep down, some primitive murderous rage from their childhood, a repressed desire to kill parents or siblings. I'm not talking about tantrums. Rage is not acceptable in our society, and we seldom express it as children because we are required to be 'good', so we have to find other outlets as we mature. If it is expressed in a safe place, like a therapist's office, a good marriage or a script, then the guilt or shame about it may diminish, and so will the sadness, the depression and the need for anger management.

41. Comedy is an outlet for rage, a way to say or do things that 'shouldn't' be said or done.

Many people to whom rage is forbidden, and who are powerless to express it for personal or cultural reasons, or both, turn it against themselves. Shame is the result. This shame, in turn, causes profound sadness. In a psychological nutshell, this is why some people who are aggressive, or prone to depression, melancholy and despair become comedians: they are trying to express their rage in a way that doesn't make them feel guilty.

Thus anger can be healthier than sadness. But it runs the big risk of upsetting people. This is why it is usually transmuted into comedy. It's safer that way.

For most people who do it professionally, comedy is an outlet for anger but not, unfortunately, a cure. They are usually unaware of it: the rage is displaced into mother-in-law jokes, spouse jokes ('Take my wife. Please.') and jokes against all institutions of society.

42. Comedy attacks the institutions of society.

Comedy makes fun of marriage, in-laws, the family, the courts, the police, the military, the Church, academia, the prison system, politicians and everyone in public life. Art is criticism of life, and comedy is criticism by ridicule.

43. Comedy is necessarily cruel.

But here's the paradox: comedians and writers of comedy enjoy being cruel but they also want to be liked. They want praise and approval. And, in purely practical terms, it's no good being the funniest person in the world if there is no audience to entertain. If a tree falls in a forest and there's no one there to see it, did it really fall?

Comedian Henny Youngman's version of this famous

philosophical conundrum is: If a husband is alone in a forest, is he still wrong? (An angry joke if ever there was one.)

Here are some more of his one-liners: 'Why do men die before their wives? They want to.' 'Why does divorce cost so much? It's worth it.'

Women also make angry jokes. About fake orgasms, Joan Rivers said: 'It's common courtesy. He's doing most of the work, you've got to encourage him.'

Comedy writers know, either instinctively or consciously, that they have to keep their rage and their despair under wraps. It must come out in their work as funny, not angry.

44. An angry *character* can be very funny. But an angry show, with few exceptions, is not.

It is merely uncomfortable.

We all know that if we are in the audience at a bad play, it is an embarrassment. I sometimes find that I have to look away from the stage, rather than watch people humiliating themselves. This is because I am in the same room as the actors who are embarrassing me and probably embarrassing themselves. It may be a big room, with a thousand seats in it, but it's still a room and I am still in it with them. I am a part of that aggressive beast, the audience, and I'd rather not be.

This doesn't seem to apply to film. I can see a bad movie without suffering any embarrassment. This is because it's been made already, it's in the past, the actors are not in the same room with me. Unless, that is, I am at a premiere; premieres have the potential to be really embarrassing occasions.

By the way, you might be perplexed when people who don't like your comedy play or film get angry. People get inexplicably angry and abusive if they expect to laugh at your show and then they don't find it funny. This doesn't happen with straight plays, but rage and aggression are inextricably tied to comedy, even including the response of a disappointed audience.

* * *

The week I graduated from Cambridge, I was wondering vaguely what I would do next and I got a phone call from Bill Oddie. 'Listen,' he said. '*Cambridge Circus* is going to Broadway. And first it's going on a tour of New Zealand. I've spoken to Humph and the others, and they want to know if you'd like to join us.'

It was a no-brainer. I had always wanted to be an actor. Here, miraculously, was a job offer, and I hadn't even left Cambridge yet.

45. At the start of your career, take any job you can get.

My first job was lucky, though to begin with it looked barely professional. The plan was to go to Yorkshire, rehearse at the house of a friend of John Cleese and Humphrey Barclay (the director), play a few performances in their private theatre – *private theatre?* – then fly to New Zealand for a pre-Broadway tour. 'Why?' I wondered, having read *Act One* by Moss Hart and many other theatrical memoirs. Why not Boston, New Haven or Philadelphia, all of which I knew were more traditional choices for a New York try-out than Christchurch, New Zealand?

Ours not to reason why; I was just an actor. I headed for Yorkshire and my first encounter with the peerage, for it turned out that John's and Humph's friend was the Hon. Jamie Dugdale, son of Lord Crathorne, a Tory peer.

The Crathorne family address was splendidly Wodehousian: Lord and Lady Crathorne, Crathorne Hall, Crathorne, Yorkshire. The driveway was about a mile long, at the end of which was a vast country pile built in around 1900. The house itself was incomplete: originally planned as a main building plus two wings, it became clear after the first wing was built that they already had more bedrooms than they could count – roughly sixty-five – plus an uncountable number of other rooms. 'My in-laws had more money than sense,' said Lady Crathorne as she hauled herself out of her low, fast Jaguar, 'and we've got more sense than money.'

I discovered that Jeff, the butler, had unpacked my battered old suitcase. This was a humiliation, as there were holes in my socks and underpants. Most of them had disappeared from my bedroom and I assumed they'd been consigned to the outer darkness, but the next day they were back in my room, darned and mended, without a word spoken. Jeff had been with the family for thirty years. He had been His Lordship's valet, but valeting went out of style and there had to be staff cuts, so, with stiff upper lip, he became the butler too. A few months later, she told me, he approached Lady Crathorne in great distress and announced that he wished to hand in his notice because he was not giving satisfaction to the houseguests.

Lady Crathorne was astonished. 'I haven't had any complaints.'

'I've had to spend so much time in the dining room, Madam,' said Jeff, 'that I haven't had time to iron the guests' shoelaces.'

Lady Crathorne managed to reassure him. She was a

friendly, charming, commonsensible woman in spite of her assumption that all civilised people voted Tory and that the government was virtually infallible. 'Cabinet ministers work frightfully hard, that's why they occasionally make mistakes. It's just tiredness, that's all.'

I was impressed that everyone except Lady Crathorne called the butler Jeff. It was so friendly and informal. 'Hi, Jeff,' I greeted him cheerily at every meal. Then a rather embarrassed Humphrey informed me quietly that his surname was Jeff and that I should have been addressing him as *Mr* Jeff; instead of being friendly, I'd been condescending. It was nice of Humphrey to give me a heads-up, in breach of the old rule, 'A good chap doesn't tell a good chap what a good chap ought to know.' I suppose it was obvious that I wasn't a good chap. Concerned, I went to find Mr Jeff in the pantry early the next morning to apologise, and found him ironing the newly arrived copy of the *Daily Telegraph*. I asked him why. 'To remove the creases, sir,' he said, 'and so that it's not too cold for His Lordship to pick up.' It was July.

We rehearsed for three days in the vast echoing ballroom and then we played our two shows in the Georgian Theatre at Richmond, a tiny but beautiful 230-seat theatre, perfectly restored to look exactly as it did in 1788. Afterwards we all adjourned to a stately home belonging to the Marquess and Marchioness of Zetland, driving through a gateway the size of Marble Arch to a party described as small and informal, which meant that you helped yourself to strawberries and champagne instead of being served by the flunkeys. The Countess of Rosse told me that my Welsh preacher monologue was the most brilliant thing in the show, and I decided that Lord Snowdon's mummy couldn't possibly be wrong.

After one week, I was liking show business quite a lot. The first leg of the Broadway try-out had gone extremely well.

We flew to New Zealand on the now defunct BOAC. Graham Chapman had returned to the company on leave from Bart's medical school and he explained carefully to us all that, as we would be in the air for twenty-four hours, we should take one of the powerful sleeping pills that he had thoughtfully brought for us so we would all arrive rested and refreshed. Gratefully we each took a pill and fell asleep as we lifted off from Heathrow. An hour and a half later we landed at Frankfurt and had to get off the plane. Then we landed at Beirut, Karachi, Calcutta, Singapore, Perth and Sydney, forced to disembark each time, still completely drugged, eyeballs rolling up into our heads. At Sydney we changed planes for Melbourne and again at Melbourne for Auckland. It took nearly two weeks to regain full consciousness. Remember:

46. Avoid drugs. They may help you be funny by removing your inhibitions; they will also ruin your life.

Everywhere we landed the heat was intense. Karachi airport men's room had no hot water. Calcutta proudly advertised 'Air-Conditioned Lounge', which turned out to mean a couple of lazy, creaking ceiling fans. There were flies everywhere. Bill Oddie, ever the ornithologist, pointed out vultures circling around the concrete airstrip. It was an omen.

It had been summer in England but it was mid-winter when we arrived in New Zealand. We hadn't thought of that. In grey and colourless Christchurch we were met by grey and colourless Mr Seeger, representing the producer Sir Robert Kerridge. We were driven to the Stonehurst Hotel, which had the standard of comfort associated with a bad youth hostel or a good public school. It smelled of damp, linoleum and suet pudding. My bedroom was six feet by ten, about a foot larger than a prison cell (I'm told), and was very cold. It had a single bed and a small chest of drawers with chipped white paint. It had no key, and efforts to get one from Reception were in vain. Valuables could be deposited with her, explained the crone behind the counter.

47. Check out digs in advance. Now we have the internet, this is easy.

The Stonehurst was a temperance establishment. None of us were pleased about that, particularly Graham Chapman. The rooms, an endless number of tiny cubby holes with plywood walls, were so arranged that all the male guests were at the back of the hotel and all the females at the front. They were plainly determined to keep us on the straight and narrow. Not that we could have moved from room to room in the night without the danger of hypothermia. No en suite bathrooms, of course: there was one room marked *MEN*, with one bath, two lavatories and two showers; one toilet in this luxurious establishment had no lock on the door, the other a lock but no light so it couldn't be shut.

We were invited to drinks at Mr Seeger's hotel, the Embassy, which had a liquor licence and was warm and well staffed. He made a sentimental speech about how nice, warm and friendly all New Zealanders are. Our hearts were untouched. We learned that Robert Kerridge, who imported us, had seen the show in London but had absolutely no recollection of it; Mr Seeger was under the impression we were some kind of real circus and didn't know why there were so few of us.

49

Back at the Stonehurst, the outside temperature was plunging. The rooms were unimaginably cold. Graham lit a small fire in an ashtray beside his bed, got into bed and lay there puffing furiously at his pipe with his hands clasped around the warm bowl, muttering that he'd really rather live in a tent. Then he realised that his bed was damp – in fact, wet. I checked mine – it was mildewed. Up early next morning due to the prevailing sogginess, I met Humphrey and Bill in the Dining Room. The waitress, an anaemic, sniffling blonde waif, brought over the menu. The first item said *Fruit or Prunes*.

'What's the fruit?' I asked.

'Prunes,' she said.

Several more of our party arrived but were not allowed to sit with any of us who were already eating. They were spaced out at different tables all over the room. You had to sit on a chair that corresponded to your room number. Tim Brooke-Taylor came down last, sat down with Jo Kendall and Graham, and was told that if he didn't move to his correct seat he wouldn't get any breakfast. So he sat by himself at another table some distance away, ordered egg and bacon, and was rewarded with a plate of sausages and gravy. 'That's all we've got left,' said the waitress, and departed.

I went out walking. Christchurch was the third-biggest town in New Zealand but it felt like a very small town indeed, more like the American south than England: many wooden houses, often neo-Georgian in style with pointless pillars; no two buildings were alike on any street; most businesses were one or two storeys, with huge neon signs on the roofs; and there was an immense number of cheap eating places, smelling of lard. All the roads were laid out on a parallel grid. The comedian Vic Oliver had caused grave offence shortly before we were there. On leaving the town he was asked how he liked it. 'Christchurch is very well laid out,' he said. 'How long has it been dead?'

Humphrey was busy lighting at the Majestic Cinema. This wasn't easy because the set was still being built. By the time he tried to start the technical rehearsal at 7pm it was clear that the mics didn't work, the wardrobe mistress had gone home at five o'clock, members of the band were having trouble playing in the same key and time signature as each other, and the stage manager had never stage-managed a show in his life. Mr Seeger and the Kerridge organisation had spared all expense.

48. Don't trust producers you don't know.

Humphrey kept his temper in the face of all the odds. The opening performance was approaching. Ron, chief electrician, looked at his watch and remarked sagely, 'Six o'clock. It gets late early.'

We opened to a full house of fourteen hundred students. Humphrey was in the stage-management corner, running the show. Though Ron was late on all his lighting cues, the audience laughed a lot. The following morning there was no review in *The Press*: the sub-editor left it out by mistake. It was printed the following morning and it seemed to be a rave: 'Sometimes satric and forever runny,' was the summing up. We presumed these were typos but by now we were certain of little.

John Cleese moved out to the Embassy Hotel. Since *Cambridge Circus* had closed in the West End he'd had a job at BBC Radio writing scripts for the comedian Dick Emery, so he had the kind of money that got you a better class of hotel in Christchurch, New Zealand.

By the weekend we'd gone from half-full houses to full ones. On Sunday we flew to Dunedin, over uninhabited foothills, Mount Cook and the spectacular Southern Alps. The sea was like green frosted glass, the white caps seeming not to move; it was like flying over a still photograph. Dunedin, so called because it was said to be 'a mixture' of Dundee and Edinburgh, was slightly more welcoming than Christchurch. The Leviathan Hotel had no bar either, but it had a coffee lounge and – joy of joys – heaters in the bedrooms.

Our show was devastatingly new. Preceding us on the Kerridge-Odeon circuit were *Paris by Night* and *The Black and White Minstrel Show*, both with leggy Australian chorus girls and one or two imported lead actors. Revue meant 'leg show', and our legs weren't causing much excitement. Here is a sample poster:

There are no animals in this circus
but the fun is
animal size –
it's a **whale** of a laugh and you'll
applaud till you're as weak as a **kitten**.
Not gee-gee but hee-hee!
Not wo-wo but ho-ho!
Not baa-baa but ha-ha!
It's all healthy hilarious horseplay at the
CAMBRIDGE CIRCUS

Mr Seeger wasn't taking any chances.

49. In your contract, try to get approval of, or consultation about, publicity and marketing.

Consultation means that they show you after they've made their decisions. 'Meaningful consultation' means they show you when they think they've made their decisions. Approval means approval.

50. Consider how to market a show before you create it, not after.

I made a film with Steve Martin called *Sgt Bilko*.[12] Steve is a delightful man and a uniquely original comedian. I loved working with him, but the film itself was a dreadful marketing mistake: it was made without a target audience. The original TV series had been popular ten years after World War II and only three years after the Korean War, and every man in America knew then what it was like to be in the army; but by the time we made the film there was no conscription and only a small professional army. There was no recognition. No owning up. A basic error. (See Rules 15 and 16.)[13]

No one realised the marketing mistake. I should have, but I didn't. Nor did Brian Grazer, the producer. The Universal marketing department should have, but give them a script with a hot star and a hot producer attached and they'll make it, whatever it is.

I should have noticed something was wrong with Universal's marketing department. I had just made a film, *Greedy*,

---

12 In America, unlike Britain, the TV show on which it was based has not been shown on TV for many years, and very few members of the public have any recollection of the great Phil Silvers, the original Bilko.
13 And that wasn't the only problem. It also had no hideous dilemma and the stakes were far too low.

written by Lowell Ganz and Babaloo Mandel, which I liked and still like. Michael J. Fox and Kirk Douglas starred in it. Michael was a big star when the deal was made but, in the meantime, three films of his had come out and not done well – so Universal refused to sell it as a Michael J. Fox film. Instead, they buried his name in a bunch of small print on the posters and ads, amongst all the other actors who, though excellent, were not movie stars. I asked why. The head of marketing said to me: 'I have two words for you about how we are going to market this film: en semble.'

That's when I should have started wondering about Universal's marketing.

* * *

Meanwhile, the purveyors of the healthy hilarious horseplay were not getting along so well in New Zealand. After three weeks of togetherness, cracks were starting to appear. No work was being done to improve the show. Everyone seemed very relaxed about Broadway. I was not. I had been to New York.

Humph finally saw the need for rehearsal, and he gave a little speech in the hotel lounge explaining that the joyride was over, and from now on we would start working properly for the New York opening. John, as always, derided him as 'the Head Pre' (Humphrey had been Head Boy of Harrow), just in case Humphrey was under the impression that he was in charge. It was obvious to John that John was in charge.

51. Comedy groups, like rock bands, are riven with rivalry, dissension and ill-feeling.

Egotistical struggles for control were starting up all around me. It was like being back at school. Nobody listened to me because I was the new boy. Lunch that day was followed by a lazy matinee, which Humph watched from out front and denounced as amateurish and awful. He was right.

On Sunday we left the South Island of New Zealand for ever. We were excited about Wellington, the capital, because we were booked into the Beverly Hills Hotel. We had underestimated Kerridge: this Beverly Hills Hotel, unlike its more famous counterpart, had no heaters *or* washbasins in the rooms – in fact, there were two washbasins, one bath and one shower in one communal space serving eighteen bedrooms. It was a lot less cosy than an army barracks. We couldn't get into any other hotel because of an international trade fair in the town.

The theatre that night was virtually full, about fourteen or fifteen hundred people, the audience much more sophisticated, and the reviews the next day were enthusiastic. Afterwards we were presented to the Governor-General of New Zealand, a retired British general wearing a monocle, and his very tall, thin wife, who had sat in the front row centre of the dress circle, which had a Union Jack draped over the front of it. We had to bow.

We left picturesque little Wellington for our final stop in Auckland, the biggest city, near the north of the North Island. Huge landlocked harbours and two volcanic mountains *in* the town. The theatre was another badly converted cinema with no atmosphere, but the audience and the press loved us, especially Bill, so John wasn't pleased. There was much talk about how to improve it for Broadway but little action; too much arrogance. We had yet to make the show consistently funny from start to finish. I was fine; I had no complaint because to me it was a job, a world trip, a stay in New York and a great adventure.

On the last weekend Bill, David and Ann Hatch and I drove to Rotorua, the thermal volcanic area in the middle of the North Island. The smell of rotten eggs was overpowering. All the volcanic activity took the form of escaping hydrogen sulphide, hence the stink. Nauseated, we hurried into a restaurant for lunch, straight into the other, more familiar and almost equally awful New Zealand smell – fried food cooked in lard. Suddenly we were overwhelmed with hysterical laughter: on our first free day in seven weeks we had come to the worst-smelling restaurant in the worst-smelling place on the planet. Venturing out again, trying not to vomit, we saw the Pohutu geyser shooting a jet of boiling water sixty feet into the air out of rock at the end of the street. It erupts irregularly. Theoretically we were fortunate to have seen it. We walked to the middle of the thermal area over hot rocks and, looking down into a six-foot-wide pit, we could see foul-smelling water frothing and boiling noisily. Jets of steam were escaping from holes in the rock all around us. Up towards the bushes near a preserved Maori village was a pool of boiling, churning mud, 180 degrees Fahrenheit. *Really* smelly.

52. A try-out or test screening should take place in front of appropriate audiences.

In other words, don't try out a Broadway show in Yorkshire or New Zealand.

The *Cambridge Circus* cast now flew to New York and

checked into the grubby, paint-flaky Chesterfield Hotel on West 49th Street, five minutes' walk from the Plymouth Theatre on 44th and Broadway. There had been virtually no advance publicity here either. Unless we were a smash hit with six raves from the six New York daily papers, we'd be gone in a week.

After the technical run-through Michael White, who had just arrived, had a hunted look about him: between them, the American producers wanted to cut ten numbers, maybe a third of the show. These included 'Regella', my monologue, written by John Cleese, because David Frost had performed it on nationwide TV without John's knowledge two days earlier. (He did this so often that Peter Cook referred to him as The Thief of BadGags.) They also insisted that we should move 'Humour without Tears', the brilliant custard pie/slapstick sketch borrowed from Michael Palin's and Terry Jones's 1963 Oxford revue, to the end of the first act. They were right.

Here is what I learned from Michael White:

53. At a preview, the producer and director have already seen the show. Now they should watch the audience too.

When are they restless? When do they cough a lot, or look at the ceiling, or their watches? Are there any walk-outs? If so, when?

54. The audience are not professionals and, although they may know that something is amiss, they probably don't know what – or how to solve the problem.

It is unlikely that members of the public can tell the symptom from the disease. You have to listen to what their *problem* is, and then reach your own conclusions about how to solve it. This rule applies not only to members of the audience but also to investors, publicists and producers' girlfriends and boyfriends, all of whom will tell you what you should do.

To take a simple example: people may say that the second act of a play is too long. It may be – but it may not be. It could be that the whole thing is too long and that the real problem lies in Act One. It may be that it's not too long but it *felt* it, perhaps because it wasn't clear and the audience didn't understand something that they needed to know.

Don't ignore the comments, though. If they're not laughing at something you think they ought to be laughing at, try to work out why. Don't say: 'I'm an artist, what do they know?' You can do that with other genres, but *the purpose of a comedy is to make the audience laugh*.

55. If the audience is expecting to laugh, whatever else you want them to derive from the performance will depend on whether or not they think it's funny.

* * *

We played our first Broadway preview of *Cambridge Circus* on a Saturday night, and the lead producer, the legendary Sol Hurok, was there in person. This was the first time he ever met Michael White. His words of greeting were: 'Why aren't you wearing a suit?' While Michael tried to think of a reply, Hurok snarled, 'I hear it's a lousy show,' and walked on into the stalls.

The first half went well enough, but the second half opened with an Oscar Wilde parody which wasn't understood, and mic trouble killed a couple of the songs. A comedy revue is all about momentum: lose the audience for thirty seconds and it's over. At the post-mortem several numbers we had cut were put back in, and others were dropped. We had now had fifty per cent of our New York previews. There was one more to go.

Next day there was more re-lighting because of the new, ever-changing running order. But that night the show was a success and there were cheers at the curtain calls. Delighted, the producers arranged a party at Sardi's for the following night.

56. Don't do much on the day of a theatre press night. Save your energy.

Opening day: we worked in the theatre, from 10am to 5pm. This was a mistake. Technical rehearsals, re-lighting, then a band call, and by five we were exhausted. All at once, it was time for the show. The thing that you've been anticipating for months and months is suddenly upon you, and over before you even realise it. At the interval, Humph came round and told us that we were sluggish and below standard. I was sure he was right.

57. Generally, notes during the interval are a bad idea. But, as I said, there are exceptions to every rule.

In this case, it undoubtedly helped.

We crossed the street to Sardi's to await the verdict. In the small upstairs room most people were drinking champagne. David Black, another of the producers, squat, dark, balding, horn-rims, burst in joyfully with news that the *Daily News* liked it. He vanished, back to a phone in a borrowed office. Ten minutes later he returned in a sombre mood: Howard Taubman in the *New York Times* had given us usable quotes but his review would not encourage people to buy tickets. Gloom enveloped the room. Unopened champagne was boxed up, ready for removal.

Apparently it now depended on Walter Kerr in the *Tribune*. If he didn't like it, all was lost. Ten minutes later David Black was back, bubbling with excitement. 'I think we're in business!' The *Trib* had called us all geniuses. The champagne was brought back. Right then – that is, shortly before midnight on opening night – we were called into a corner and asked not to take any writers' royalties if we were running at a loss for the first few weeks. (It made very little difference to me, as I had written almost nothing.) In return, David told us he would spend $80,000 on publicity, starting with a big ad in the *Times* reprinting Kerr's review. I wondered why some plan to spend money on publicity hadn't been made in advance. I thought Broadway was legendary for its know-how. Apparently not.

The evening papers, the next day, were enthusiastic. The *Post* liked it a lot, as did *The Journal-American* and *World Telegram*. We had five out of six New York dailies, but not the *Times*. Could we survive?

The following week, houses gently declined. One night I was outside the stage door, actually signing *autographs*, when a dazzling Hitchcock-blonde in a long white dress and a diamond necklace hurried towards me. 'My name is Mary Ure. I thought you were marvellous, all of you.' She and her husband Robert Shaw were on their way to Sardi's for their first-night ritual. He had just opened in Dürrenmatt's play *The Physicists*. She must have seen our show on another day. She invited me to have a drink with them before the Wednesday matinee. This was about ten years before Robert became a world-famous movie star in *The Sting*, followed by *Jaws*, but I was a fan because I'd seen him starring with my boyhood hero Peter O'Toole in Willis Hall's wonderful war play *The Long and the Short and the Tall*. Mary Ure was already the stuff of theatrical legend: previously married to John Osborne, she had originated the role of Alison in *Look Back in Anger*. I'd seen her in the film, in which she was profoundly touching. Star-struck, amazed to find myself welcomed in the company of these gods and totally unaware of the misery that lay beneath the glamorous surface, I sat in an expensive restaurant with them, nervously sipped a Coke and wondered if life could be any more exciting than this. So:

58. Don't believe other people's publicity. It's probably no more accurate than your own.

That evening David Black warned us that Hurok would give us one week's notice on Monday. David wanted to keep the show on, so he would have to raise an additional $20,000 in the next week. That Sunday we were to be guests, live, on *The Ed Sullivan Show*. If the bookings picked up after that, he would do it.

Ed Sullivan hosted the NBC Sunday night variety show. He couldn't sing, dance or tell jokes, but he was a star. He had been an avid supporter of the right-wing McCarthy witch-hunt. He was sternly Catholic and moralistic. 'Ed Sullivan will be around as long as someone else has talent,' the comedian Fred Allen famously remarked. His programme was the best publicity anyone could get. He had been to see *Cambridge Circus* and had loved it, but he refused to allow us to do 'Hallelujah!', an ingenious parody of the Beatles singing the Hallelujah Chorus, which would have been perfect for his show since he had introduced the Beatles to America less than a year earlier. Instead, he opted for a parody of a hot gospel song called 'London Bus', which I had never liked, especially as in New York the racial tension was pervasive.

The word 'black' was itself potentially explosive; to describe someone as black in 1964 was as bad as using 'nigger' today. Black didn't become the word of choice until the Black Panthers came on the scene in the late sixties, with their defiant slogan 'Black is beautiful!' Everyone I knew, liberals all, were so careful not to cause offence that, when they were being served by an African-American waitress in a coffee shop, they wouldn't order black coffee – they would ask for 'coffee without cream'. Maybe I was over-sensitive because nobody but me seemed bothered by the song. My real problem with it was that I didn't think it funny; jokes that touched on racism had to be good. For instance, in January 1965, just before I left New York, there was an item on the news: a negro in Mississippi had just been found with twelve bullet holes in him. Cleese remarked that it was the worst case of suicide the deep south had ever had.

Ed Sullivan also selected a mime in which Graham Chapman wrestled with himself, and a mime that I did using a banana as a gun. Walter Kerr had written, 'I cherish the sight of Jonathan Lynn reloading a banana. I have never seen a banana reloaded before.' There had been a photo of me, firing the banana, in *Time* magazine the week after we opened on Broadway, and now I was making my TV debut on the biggest show in America, probably in the world. It was hard to believe. I was three months out of Cambridge and I was almost famous. I've been almost famous several times in my life, without ever surmounting that last hurdle. My heart wasn't in it. I preferred privacy.

We got bad news as soon as we arrived at the CBS Theatre[14] on that Sunday morning. Kruschev's regime in the Kremlin had just fallen. This was only two years after the Cuban missile crisis. *Dr Strangelove* had been released that year. Fear of the Soviet Union was at its height. President Lyndon B. Johnson decided to address the nation for fifteen minutes at 8.30pm. This meant that fifteen minutes of *The Ed Sullivan Show*, which was live from eight until nine, would not be seen in New York. Whoever was on the air from 8.30 to 8.45 would be seen only on the West Coast and in Canada. If that's when we went on, *Cambridge Circus* would almost certainly close; we needed that vital injection of publicity in New York.

59. Where possible, avoid clashes with world-shaking events. They are bad for business. (See Rule 31.)

The other acts on the bill were The Animals, performing their new hit record 'The House of the Rising Sun'; Joan Sutherland performing *her* hit song, the mad scene from *Lucia di Lammermoor*; Rita Pavone, a sixteen-year-old Italian rock star performing an Italian hit song that none of us ever heard of, before or since; Jackie Mason, the Brooklyn rabbi turned stand-up comedian; and, with top billing, Van Johnson, ageing movie star, singing 'The Girl from Ipanema' from his cabaret at the Copacabana.

The morning was spent on camera blocking and orchestra calls. The dress rehearsal started three-quarters of an hour

---

14   It's the one they use now for *The David Letterman Show*.

late because the theatre was besieged by thousands of screaming twelve-year-old girls and The Animals couldn't get back
in after lunch. It had a full audience of twelve hundred, also
mostly teenage girls. When Van Johnson walked across the
stage, none of them recognised him or knew that only fifteen
years earlier he had been a famous heart-throb. Ozymandias.

As we were even less famous than Rita Pavone, whoever
she was, we were placed in the 8.35 spot, and David Black
told us that we had to pull out all the stops at the dress rehearsal if we wanted our time slot changed. So we gave it
everything we had. Overall the dress rehearsal went badly
and overran by half an hour, partly because Jackie Mason's act
was ad libbed and he tried one joke after another, determined to find a few thoughts that this adolescent audience would
find funny. But in vain.

60. Don't try to sing a song on live TV unless you know the lyrics.

Everybody else's acts were either long or bad. Van Johnson,
standing in the middle of a chain of swirling, leggy showgirls
wearing wafty costumes, sang

> When she walks she's like a samba
> That swings so cool and sways so gentile ...

The prop man, Jewish no doubt, had written 'gentile' instead
of 'gentle' on the idiot cards, and of course Van Johnson sang
it.

A tension-filled wait followed the dress rehearsal. Word
came down from the glass control box that the show was
being 're-routined'. Some people would be substantially

trimmed or maybe cut altogether. People hung around in an uneasy silence. Finally, the changes were announced: the first half-hour would include songs from The Animals and one song from Rita Pavone (her second song was cut). Joan Sutherland's aria (already trimmed from twenty minutes to eight) was now down to four minutes. Van Johnson's big number was cut entirely, though he was offered a chance to do a different song while President Johnson was on the air. Jackie Mason was now topping the bill (or finishing the show, anyway).

We had done so well at the dress rehearsal that we were re-scheduled for 8.25. More than half of our stuff would be seen before the President came on, and we would be seen by the highest possible number of viewers – Ed Sullivan's usual audience plus all the extra people tuning in to hear the President. Considering that we were the only act not billed outside the theatre, we were pretty happy.

Van Johnson was not. He put on his fedora and walked out. His agent and manager followed him, pleading with him not to offend the great and powerful Sullivan. He was persuaded to return and a compromise was reached, whereby Ed would introduce him at 8.11pm. and tell viewers that they'd be seeing him sing later in the show (which was true only if they lived in Toronto or LA). Ed introduced himself momentarily to me, and asked that when I exited past him at the end of our 'London Bus' song, would I please give him a playful tap on the head with my tambourine?

By now we were more or less imprisoned in the theatre due to the growing mob outside. I looked briefly out of a seventh-floor window and was greeted by a burst of hysterical teenage screaming. Clearly I resembled an Animal. There was tension in the make-up room. The show started. I was about to make my very first TV appearance. Just before I went on, a stage-hand said to me: 'Do you know there's nearly seventy million people watching this?' I later learned that he often did that; it amused him to terrify the performers. When I went on, my knees shook so much I thought they wouldn't support me. I got through it, got a huge laugh with my banana gag. The audience liked our amateurish performance, and as I danced off (for want of a better word) past Ed, I gave him what was intended to be that playful tap on the head with the tambourine. Unfortunately, because of my nerves and excessive adrenalin, I smashed it down onto his head. His eyes crossed for a moment, his knees buckled, but I was gone.

This incident may not have contributed to his good temper, which didn't last out the evening.

61. Stand-up material should be different for different audiences.

When Jackie Mason went on, he found the same problem that he'd had at the dress rehearsal: the teeny-boppers out front just weren't getting his jokes. He'd been on for nearly his full ten or twelve minutes when, halfway through a long set-up for a gag, he received a two-minute signal from a stage manager. Thrown, he went all the way back to the beginning of the joke, and when he reached the same point he got a one-minute signal. These signals were in the form of two fingers, then one finger. Thrown off his stride, and perhaps panicked, Mason glanced at the stage manager and said: 'And a finger to you.'

I was watching on a monitor and, although no obscene gesture was visible, the screen was immediately blacked out. After a short pause Sullivan appeared, closing the show.

Then, as the monitors went black, I heard sounds of a fight and some shouting from across the studio.

The next day, on the front pages, I read that Sullivan had physically attacked Jackie Mason, pushed him through the studio doors and down a flight of stairs, and fired him from a six-show contract worth $45,000, big money in those days. Ed Sullivan was a powerful enemy: after that night, Mason didn't get another job on television for about fifteen years. And by the following evening it was already clear that *The Ed Sullivan Show* hadn't done the trick for us. With only slightly more activity at our box office, one week's notice was posted. The week was spent playing to small houses, and going to jazz clubs afterwards. On Thursday it was announced in the press that we were closing on Saturday. The box office was deluged. We finished the week with big houses and cheering at the end, but it was over.

Then, it wasn't over after all. A dinner theatre in the East Village called Square East, which had been the home of the Second City improv group, asked us to transfer there. A few days later we opened in a large room just off Washington Square with tables, chairs, red curtains and décor, expensive food and drink and a squad of waitresses who had perfected the art of clinking drinks or dropping cutlery on the funny lines.

62. Try to insist that drinks and food are not served while you're on the stage.

Al Murray and Charlie Rubin were the friendly and hopeful proprietors. We were to stay until January at least, come up with some new material and open it to club critics as a new show. They had no intention of interfering, they said; all they wanted was for something creative to be happening there.

Al and Charlie were doomed to disappointment. Nothing creative occurred. In the first week we played to 450 people instead of the 800 they had budgeted for. Over Thanksgiving we were packed, with enthusiastic audiences. Some nights we were nearly empty. I could see that I'd be going home in January.

I wasn't sad to leave the grubby old Chesterfield Hotel. The only thing I really liked about it was the very short Italian-American elevator man who chatted to me in the early hours when I got home. One day he saw me holding a copy of Oscar Wilde's plays. 'He was a great guy,' said the elevator man, jabbing the cover with a stubby forefinger. 'He was over here, you know.'

'When?' I said.

'I don't know, I wasn't here to greet him.'

Another night he asked me, out of the blue: 'Do you remember Sir Harry Lauder?'

'I don't remember him,' I said, 'but apparently he was a good comedian. I know his records.'

'Was he English?'

'No, Scottish.'

'Has England *ever* had any great comedians? You know, like Charlie Chaplin?'

* * *

Years later, I started writing situation-comedy episodes in collaboration with George Layton. We had both been actors in *Doctor in the House* on TV. *Doctor in Charge* was the sequel, which George was still in. One week, a script either wasn't delivered by one of the writing teams or was not accepted. George heard about this and phoned to suggest that we try to write one. His charming collection of short stories about his childhood in Bradford had been published; I had written a long-form TV play which had been bought but not produced. We realized it was an unusual opportunity to break into TV writing as we both knew all the regular characters, we knew the producer (Humphrey Barclay) and we knew he needed a script in a hurry. Then we had even more beginner's luck: somehow we wrote a really funny script. Humph loved it, the audience loved it, and he immediately commissioned us to write several more. Overnight success as a writer after trying for six years. As a result we were asked to write scripts for *On the Buses*, then a colossal hit, *My Name Is Harry Worth* and other shows.

Ronald Wolfe and Ronald Chesney, a highly successful comedy team, had created *On the Buses*. Their first big success had been *Educating Archie*, a radio show for the ventriloquist Peter Brough and his dummy Archie Andrews.[15] Chesney had started out as a harmonica player in variety and he was featured on *Educating Archie* every week as a *talking* harmonica – he actually could make a mouth organ sound as though it was talking. When I was a kid I thought it really *was* a talking harmonica. After that, they wrote several big TV hits, including *The Rag Trade*, *Meet the Wife* and *The Bed-Sit Girl*. They had what was called the common touch. George did too. Unfortunately, I didn't.

On the Buses was their biggest success of all, and for several seasons they had written every episode. Now they were going

15 A ventriloquist on the radio? Yes, and at the age of nine I was taken to see him for my birthday at the Bristol Hippodrome. His lips moved visibly every time Archie Andrews spoke. My parents explained that was why he needed radio to make him a star.

to write and produce several feature films based on the series, so new writers were needed to keep the show on the air. The Ronnies started out by explaining their first strict rule: no more than 140 speeches in each show. Why? 'Because that's the speed the actors go at. Don't write more than that, it's a waste of time, it'll just get cut.'

I suggested that if we wrote more perhaps they would go faster, which I privately thought would be a great improvement. 'No,' they said. 'Won't work. They won't go faster. They never go faster. Hundred and forty speeches. You'll see.'

The show concerned a bus driver, Reg Varney, and a bus conductor, Bob Grant, who spent most of their time chatting up 'clippies' – female bus conductors – at the Depot, where the bane of their existence was Inspector Blake. The episodes essentially took place either at the Depot or at home, where the characters were Reg's dumb sister Olive, his morose brother-in-law and his mum.

63. If writing about something outside your experience, research.

Although, like most people, I was a bus passenger from time to time, I knew nothing about buses or bus depots. And, foolishly, I hadn't bothered to research. Ronnie Wolfe asked me if we had any ideas for stories, and I had lots. This was around the time that hijacking planes became an epidemic. 'What about some terrorists hijacking the bus?' I said. 'They hold Reg and Bob hostage. Maybe Mum or Olive is on the bus too. And the passengers form a microcosm of society – you know, a pregnant woman, a German physicist, a cockney sparrow who plays his harmonica to keep everybody's spirits up . . .'

Ronnie Wolfe interrupted me. 'No, no, Jon,' he said, kindly but puzzled. 'See, they don't hijack buses, Jon, they hijack planes.'

'Yes, I know that, but . . .'

I could see that it wasn't worth pursuing for now. I turned to women's liberation, also tremendously in vogue, and another idea so preposterous in the context of *On the Buses* that I was sure it would be funny. 'What if Olive becomes a supporter of women's lib and burns her bra?'

The Ronnies Wolfe and Chesney glanced at each other. *Is this man sane?* the look seemed to say. Ronnie Wolfe carefully explained again: 'No, Jon, you see, the thing is, women's lib is a middle-class fad. This is a workin' class show. What we want is jokes about the price of fish.'

I had no idea how to go about writing jokes about the price of fish. After that meeting everything in my life looked grey. A depression took hold and sapped my energy, closing down my brain. I needed to play with ideas in order to be funny, and the mere thought of attempting jokes about the price of fish created a sense of terminal inertia. I was chronically exhausted. I couldn't get up in the mornings. I wanted to get out of the job but we had a big new mortgage. I also felt I couldn't let George down. George couldn't see a problem.

So, laboriously, we worked out some storylines, George doing far more than his share, got them approved and eventually sent in our first draft script. The Ronnies had explained to us that if they found anything funny they would put a tick by it in the margin. The first script was rapidly returned to us with a terse note attached: 'Not enough ticks.'

It was true. When we looked at it there were very few ticks, certainly not enough. On the other hand, George and I felt that we had written many funny lines and moments that had somehow gone *un*-ticked. So we ticked all the jokes that we thought had been overlooked, and sent it back. We heard no more about ticks.

64. When writing to a brief, just grin and bear it. Most of us have to go through this. It's experience, it's good training, and it's paid.

Five times more we went through this agonising process, trying to extract laughs from stories about nothing. I think Wolfe and Chesney must have found it equally hard, dealing with this tiresome writer who wasn't really in tune with their show, though they were unfailingly gracious and courteous. At our first rehearsal we had the temerity to give the cast a script of 150 speeches. Wolfe and Chesney were proved right – the show overran by ten speeches. After that, as we wrote, I kept counting the speeches to see how close we were to 140 and finishing the bloody thing! Never have I felt so desperate to get to the end of writing anything. Yet when the shows were recorded, they seemed sort of funny, and our first episode received, of all things, an enthusiastic notice in *The Times*, a pompous, stuffy newspaper in those days. Disappointingly for us, the critic credited Wolfe and Chesney with our script. It would have been our first review.

One day I asked the Ronnies if Reg Varney's house had a back garden, because it would help the story we were working on. They thought back over many shows. 'No, no, I don't think we've ever established a garden. It's still an option.' The Ronnies taught me many useful tricks of the trade, like that one:

65. When writing a series, keep your options open. Never commit yourself to anything until you have to.

George Layton and I continued work on the *Doctor* series. I think we wrote twenty-five episodes in all, but it became frustrating to me after a while. I had wanted to expand its horizons and make it both more real and more satirical. It had been okay for the series to be mainly japes, wheezes and practical jokes when it was about medical students, but as the principal characters became doctors I felt it was time for the series to grow up too.

66. More jeopardy equals more comedy.

I proposed episodes in which the doctors amputated the wrong leg, and another in which Professor Loftus was wholly in favour of vivisection until his own cat was dissected by mistake. Humphrey Barclay was determined that we shouldn't alarm the great British public about their health service. I couldn't see why not. I thought it would be a thoroughly good thing, actually, so long as it was funny and based on truth. I didn't subscribe to the popular notion that comedy must always reassure the audience, and I still don't. The essential Hideous Dilemma must drive the story even if the ending is comforting.

I found compromises with Humph but I felt the scripts were less funny than they might have been. Of course, I might easily have been wrong about that. It was never tested. However:

67. Do what the producer says unless you don't mind being fired.

Some jeopardy was allowed to enter into the *Doctor* stories, but there was always a reassuring denouement. George had always been willing to go along with my satirical ideas, although temperamentally he was, I think, more in tune with Humphrey's cosier approach.

We decided the time had come to create our own TV show and act in it ourselves. The idea came from a well-known experiment that I had heard about at Cambridge when I was reading some criminology. Twin studies were used in an attempt to discover if criminal behaviour was caused by genetics or upbringing – the famous 'nature versus nurture' question – and the researchers managed to find the missing identical twin brothers of thirteen persistent criminal offenders, or recidivists. The result was startling: of the thirteen missing twins who were found, nine were also recidivists. The other four were policemen.

We called our series *My Brother's Keeper*. As it developed, it somehow moved away from my original satirical thought, which was to examine the proposition that law-breakers and law-enforcers are psychologically close. Granada Television didn't quite have the courage of my convictions. They felt that a criminal would be too unsympathetic as one of the brothers, and in my desire for success and anxiety to please I was easily persuaded. We made the petty criminal into a student and an anarchist, a readily recognisable type in the heady days of student revolution in 1973. That was a mistake, as it both confused and compromised the basic theme.

This lack of clarity was my fault. I failed to hold on

strongly enough to my original notion. Whenever I have allowed that to happen the result has not been good.

68. Rule 67 applied to work for which you have been hired. On a project that you create, don't be pressured into betraying your original comic notion.

We had both been great fans of *Whatever Happened to the Likely Lads?*, by Dick Clement and Ian La Frenais, two writers I admire, and our show fell under its influence, becoming a gentler programme about working-class brothers who didn't see eye to eye. It was funny, but not sufficiently new or different.

I think George and I must have been pretty hard to handle. I played the student and George played the cop. Our producer/director Bill Podmore was a good-natured man of almost limitless patience, and he needed to be because we put ourselves firmly in the driving seat. I had directed several plays by this time, and we were both full of directorial ideas for Bill and acting notes for the cast. It must have been pretty irritating for him, though he was polite enough not to show it. My hubris even extended to writing a theme song for the show, which was dreadful and makes me blush when I think about it today. It wasn't used, of course.

69. You need some 'tip-of-the-iceberg' lines.

Dick Clement has a theory that great lines reveal the tip of an iceberg beneath. An example he gives of this is in *Tootsie*: Dustin Hoffman plays an actor who cannot get work because he is so difficult and argumentative. In desperation he goes to read for a middle-aged woman's part in a soap opera. He goes in drag, of course, auditions brilliantly and gets the part; still in drag, he then meets his agent in the Russian Tearoom on 57th Street. The agent slowly recognises him, and says, 'I begged you to get help.' This tip-of-the-iceberg line reveals a whole world of information about their relationship, and about how deeply crazy the agent thinks the actor is.

My favourite example of a tip-of-the-iceberg line comes from real life. An exhausted and gloomy Bill Podmore, at the end of a day's work with us on *My Brother's Keeper*, said: 'I can't go for a drink with you lads after work today. I have to go home, it's my wife's wedding anniversary.'

My Brother's Keeper had a good response from most of the popular press and, as I recall, was always in the top ten shows of the week, sometimes as high as number three. Unfortunately we became the favourite Aunt Sally of the most influential TV critic of the day, Elkan Allan in the *Sunday Times*. He gave us a really hostile review to start with and then relentlessly, every Sunday, took another swipe at us in his round-up of the forthcoming week.

70. Don't take the critics too seriously, whether good or bad. Trust your own judgement.

It's best not to read reviews until long afterwards.

George and Bill sensibly attached much less importance to critics than I did, but somehow it stopped mattering to me that the public was enjoying the programme. People *I* knew read the *Sunday Times*, and I felt inexplicably squashed and ashamed, psychologically defenceless against the weekly critical three-line onslaught. Granada had commissioned a second series from us, which was to be made the following year, but by the time it was broadcast my confidence had gone: while the show was still on the air I stopped going out in the street without the disguise of a big hat and sunglasses, for fear that I'd be recognised and abused by *Sunday Times* readers and other hostile inhabitants of London N10. It was an absurd overreaction. I avoided people whenever I could. I began to think that Elkan Allan was right, the show was awful, and that I was a complete failure. In reality the show was not awful, it was very funny at times; the worst that could probably be said about it was that it was ordinary.

Elkan Allan still denounced us weekly. Granada decided not to continue after the second series, although the viewing figures were excellent. George and I felt like castaways. We had been expecting the show to run for years. We tried to come up with new ideas for shows but nothing clicked. I'm sure that was because I was so dejected. I know now that to let one person, especially a journalist, take away your confidence is stupidly self-destructive.

George was acting in a play in Cheltenham, and asked me to go down there, stay in the house he had rented and work on new ideas during the day. I did, but my heart wasn't in it. I had respect for George and had enjoyed working with him. He was a hard-working, talented collaborator and we had written some really funny scripts together. But my Cambridge friends were all doing work that seemed so much more interesting: *Monty Python* and *Fawlty Towers* had by now been on the air and revitalised TV comedy. Richard Eyre was now director of the Nottingham Playhouse and had recently brought an interesting new play, *Comedians,* to The Old Vic, starring the accomplished young actors Jonathan Pryce and Stephen Rea.

Writers of television series are sausage machines, expected to turn out a product every week that is slightly different and yet exactly the same, and unless your series has something really special at the core of it you are doomed to be a well-paid mediocrity. I had had enough. I saw an ad in *The Stage* and, inspired by Richard's example, I applied to be artistic director of the Cambridge Theatre Company. I didn't want to write or act in any more situation comedies. I left Cheltenham in the rain, and my writing partnership with George was over.

I had no idea what I was going to do. I slept a lot, and suffered all the usual symptoms of depression. My melancholy mood changed abruptly when I was offered the job at Cambridge. I was not expecting that to happen.

I was no longer a joke machine, and I felt free.

* * *

71. Find a way to get ideas.

The question that all writers are asked is 'Where do you get your ideas from?', and usually there's no real answer. Some get ideas from the newspapers. I do. I also get them just from gazing out of the window at nothing with a totally blank mind. (This comes easily to me and is how I spend much of my day.) Sometimes I get them when I'm out walking, or when driving. But where do they come from? I think that they come from programming your brain in advance, by setting it a problem and then leaving your subconscious to mull over it without your supervision. However, there are certain basics that help me:

72. The oldest source of comedy is the Ten Commandments.

This is because comedy is about the breaking of taboos. It involves saying things that are not normally said, or admitted. The Ten Commandments are the root of our society's moral and ethical rules.[16] Here they are, from the Authorised King James Version, edited for brevity. Read them and think how many comedies are based on breaking these rules. Virtually all, I would suggest.

I am the Lord thy God.
Thou shalt have no other gods before me ... thou shalt not
    bow down thyself to them, nor serve them for I the
    LORD thy God am a jealous God, visiting the iniquity of
    the fathers upon the children unto the third and fourth
    generation of them that hate me.
Thou shalt not take the name of the LORD thy God in vain.
Remember the sabbath day, to keep it holy.
Honour thy father and thy mother.
Thou shalt not kill.
Thou shalt not commit adultery.
Thou shalt not steal.
Thou shalt not bear false witness against thy neighbour.
Thou shalt not covet thy neighbour's house, thou shalt not
    covet thy neighbour's wife, nor his manservant, nor his
    maidservant, nor his ox, nor his ass, nor any thing that is
    thy neighbour's.

---

16 Curiously, although known as the Ten Commandments, they appear as seventeen commandments in Exodus and as twenty-one commandments in Deuteronomy. This has potential for a funny, anachronistic sketch.

73. The Seven Deadly Sins are present in all comedy.

For non-Catholic readers, here they are again: *Lust, Gluttony, Greed, Sloth, Anger, Envy* and *Pride*. I keep a framed copy of the Seven Deadly Sins on my desk.

A couple of them may need further explanation: Gluttony is either a sin of over-indulgence, or of status, or withholding from the needy.

Greed, also known as Avarice and Covetousness, is about the pursuit of wealth and power. (The Church knows a thing or two about that.) It would include treachery, disloyalty or deliberate betrayal, all for personal gain.

Vanity and pomposity, essential qualities for characters in comedy, are presumably subsections of the sin of Pride.

There are some other useful comic sins that are not specifically mentioned among the Seven Deadlies: hypocrisy, cowardice and miserliness. Without these three, many comedians would have had no act: I'm thinking specifically of Jack Benny, Bob Hope and Woody Allen, each of whom based his persona on these three universally understood failings.

Jack Benny's defining joke was the scene when he was held up by a mugger at gunpoint. 'Your money or your life,' demanded the mugger.

Benny stared at him and did not speak.

The mugger started to lose patience. 'I said, your money or your life!'

'I'm thinking. I'm thinking!' said Benny.

I didn't get the idea for *Yes Minister* by staring out of the window, going for a walk or contemplating the Seven Deadly Sins. I got it from Tony Jay.

74. The best way to get good ideas is to work with somebody who has them.

* * *

Some years earlier, while writing sitcom scripts with George, John Cleese phoned to say he was starting a company called Video Arts to make management-training films, 'with a nice chap called Antony Jay', and would I mind acting with him in the first one for thirty quid plus a deferred fee? The film was going to cost over four thousand pounds. It doesn't sound like much now, but in 1969 or 1970 you could have bought a four-bedroom house in Muswell Hill for that. Feeling sorry for John, who had obviously got himself involved in some foolish scheme, I agreed immediately. It was called *Who Sold You This, Then?* When I received my deferred fees only a few months later, plus an offer to act in the next short film, it was most unexpected.

The idea behind the company was brilliantly simple. Tony Jay knew that businesses, large and small, spent money on training their staff, and that all the bigger companies had training departments with their own budgets: money that *had* to be spent every year. Mostly it was spent on renting boring training films. Tony wondered why these films couldn't be entertaining. In a moment of inspiration, he realised that training films were dull because they showed the right way to do things; if they showed the *wrong* way, they could be funny. Fortunes can be made from simple but original thoughts, plus a lot of hard work. By the time Tony, John and the other partners sold the company seventeen years later it was worth between forty and fifty million pounds.

Tony had been a successful BBC TV producer. He went there straight from Cambridge, where he gained a First in Classics, and rapidly rose to being the Editor of *Tonight* with Cliff Michelmore. Subsequently he was Head of Talks/ Features, where among the shows he was in at the start of was the legendary *That Was The Week That Was*. At the age of thirty-three he decided that he no longer wanted to work fourteen-hour days, plus nights, and weekends. 'If I can't support my family working from nine to five, Monday to Friday, there's something wrong with me.' He left, became a full-time writer, and wrote two landmark books about management: *Management and Machiavelli* and *Corporation Man*, the first of which was also a huge best-seller.

The original four thousand pounds was Tony's. When I met him on the set on the first day of a two-day shoot he was extremely agreeable. He was tall with thinning, wispy, long, greying hair, a tweed sports jacket, worn-down suede shoes and a characteristic, slightly knock-kneed stance. He talked very fast in a voice that became slightly squeaky when enthusiastic. He looked like a typical BBC producer or an Oxbridge don and seemed completely untroubled by the financial risk he was taking by starting this company.

I acted in the first four films for Video Arts, after which he phoned me. The company needed to make more films, but as John was starting work on a new series (it turned out to be *Fawlty Towers*) Tony asked Denis Norden and me to write for them. I was flattered to be in such company. Tony and I wrote about twenty scripts together. Usually I was the only credited writer, but it would have been impossible without Tony's guidance: they were difficult because every joke had to be connected to a lesson. Nothing could be included just to get a laugh. I had to study all the relevant management theory for each script, which later stood me in good stead at the Cambridge Theatre Company.

The CTC was subsidised by the Arts Council, based at the Arts Theatre in Cambridge but touring every production to middle-scale theatres in England and Wales. It was a poorly remunerated job, however, and it was clear that we would need extra income if we were to keep up the payments on our house and our son's school fees. Before I took the job Tony Jay told me that things were going so well at Video Arts that they would certainly need two or three scripts a year from me if I had the time, and with that insurance policy I said yes.

Tony also mentioned an idea that he had for a situation comedy about the civil service, set in Whitehall, and asked me if I'd write it with him. I thought it sounded boring. Furthermore, I had just renounced sitcom writing. I told him that I wasn't interested.

* * *

One of my favourite memories of directing at the Cambridge Theatre Company is the Restoration comedy *The Relapse*, with David Jason as Lord Foppington. I took a chance in casting him, persuaded by my old friend and his agent, Meg Poole. It was his first play, other than end-of-the-pier productions. He was very scared, but I knew it was within his grasp. Shortly after we opened in Cambridge, to an admiring review from Irving Wardle in *The Times*, I dropped in unannounced to watch a performance. To my astonishment, I saw David throw in a little tap dance in the middle of his first scene, which must have struck the Cambridge audience as odd, given that the play is set in about 1665.

I went round to his dressing room in the interval, and

asked why on earth he was doing time-steps after the funny lines. He was slightly indignant. 'I was workin' the house,' he said.

Which leads me to:

75. Make the comedy appropriate to the situation.

I took over the CTC in January 1977. My predecessor had not left me much money in the year's budget, just enough for two small-cast spring productions. I decided to open with *The Glass Menagerie*, which has a cast of only four. I knew that we could only attract big houses on tour by interesting casting and I had an inspiration: Connie Booth, famous from *Fawlty Towers*, was American and perfect for the role of Laura. The play is autobiographical, about a family of three in St Louis who have been abandoned by their husband and father, as were Tennessee Williams, his mother and his sister Rose.

Rose had a lobotomy in real life, but in the play she is handicapped by a limp. Connie had a quality of fragility and vulnerability which I thought would make her performance of the lame, introverted daughter unusually touching. Beyond that, one of the most interesting things about the play is that, damaged though she is, Laura is the only one in the family who is strong enough to handle the truth; Connie also personifies determination and some sort of inner certainty. The young man who narrates the play is called Tom, which was Tennessee's real name, and for this part I was able to cast James Aubrey, a young English actor who had lived and trained in America. For Amanda I got Maxine Audley, a great beauty, now slightly fading, who was high and dry after a big career in the fifties and who had famously originated the dictum 'Adultery on location doesn't count.'

When I say she was high and dry, I don't mean it literally. High, yes; dry, no. I was startled on the first day of rehearsal when promptly at twelve noon she opened her capacious handbag, yanked out a new bottle of vodka, unscrewed the top and glugged down what looked to me like a quadruple. I had heard tales of her drinking but I had not quite expected this. However, it appeared to make no difference whatever to her work, and public drinking was a lot healthier and more controllable than secret drinking. It also seemed to be in the spirit of the playwright.

When I started the production I assumed it would be completely unnoticed, just another repertory production. Once again, however, I had beginner's luck. It started with the set, which was a work of genius by Saul Radomsky, with only two thousand five hundred pounds in his budget. Saul knew of a large number of long thin transparent plastic tubes that were lying around somewhere, and used them to form what looked like a great glass cage surrounding the set. When it rained, projections made it look like water was running down the tubes. The neon signs from the offstage street reflected garish primary colours on the glass bars. Inside, the apartment itself was little more than an architectural outline of the rooms and the fire escape outside. The effect was dazzling and poetic, yet you never doubted that the apartment belonged to pitifully poor people.

Ray Cook wrote an original and beautiful score for harp and violin (two instruments were all we could afford), the rehearsals were smooth and enjoyable, but I was not expecting the national press to show up at Cambridge. They all liked it enormously, except the *Guardian*, which had a second-string critic called Nicholas de Jongh, who took me to task for allowing the play to be funny as well as touching. We were offered an immediate transfer to the Criterion Theatre in Piccadilly Circus, but Tennessee's representatives, disturbed by the *Guardian* review, refused us permission. We lost the Criterion to another play, then heard – too late – that Williams himself had read the reviews and did not object. We went to the Shaw Theatre for a limited season, not nearly as suitable a theatre but a chance to be seen in London all the same. We were in previews when I got an urgent phone call: Tennessee Williams was coming tonight, and I'd better be there in case there was trouble over my interpretation.

I hastened down to the theatre and arrived as the play began. James Aubrey spoke his opening monologue. Then Maxine swanned onto the stage, and as soon as she started talking I heard a low, deep, throaty chuckle coming from the back of the stalls. 'Heh-heh-heh!'

Several people turned around and said 'Shh!' angrily to the philistine sitting behind them. They had come to see Culture, and they knew from the *Guardian* that the play wasn't supposed to be funny.

Tennessee laughed a lot in Act One, almost too much, and I began to wonder if he was laughing *at* the production instead of with it. Nervously I introduced myself to him at the interval. I had expected a large man, a sort of Big Daddy, but I met a small fellow with big glasses and a fey Southern manner. 'I hope you don't mind the laughs that we're getting,' I said.

'Why should I? I wrote them,' he said. The comedy, it turned out, was appropriate after all.

76. There is comedy in everything, no matter how serious or 'important'.

There is comedy in *Hamlet*, *King Lear* and *Macbeth*. There can be comedy in any play or film, no matter how serious the subject or the intent. Often the laughter is a release from the tension of tragedy, an ironic counterpoint; or it can be a reminder of the depths of a character's despair, as it is throughout *Waiting for Godot*. Here again we see the thinness of the line between tragedy and comedy.

To my great joy Tennessee loved my production. He felt strongly that for Amanda to be sufficiently poignant she had to be funny, and at times slightly ridiculous. He insisted on meeting all the actors afterwards, told James Aubrey that he gave the best performance of Tom that he had ever seen and took an ad in the *Standard*, urging people to go see it. He took us all out to dinner at Joe Allen's, not once but several times. Over dinner he regaled us with anecdotes about the first production. 'You know that moment when Laura says, "A souvenir"?' he said. 'We played that completely differently.'

'You did?' I said, trying not to sound over-anxious.

'Yup. Instead of saying the line softly, gently, like Connie does here, our original Laura yelled it.' He demonstrated: 'A SOUVENIR!' People in the restaurant turned to look.

I was shocked. I thought I must have completely misunderstood Tennessee's intentions. I had supposed that this was one of the most touching moments in the play: Laura, having found that the Gentleman Caller is engaged to another girl, realises that all her romantic hopes have been mere fantasies; while having a pathetic farewell dance with him she backs clumsily into the sideboard and knocks her prized glass unicorn to the floor. It breaks. As the scene ends she picks it up, limps across the room, gives it to the Gentleman Caller and says that she wants him to have it. 'Why?' he asks. 'A souvenir,' she replies.

I asked Tennessee why the original Laura shouted the line. 'Well,' he said, 'that line "A souvenir" is Amanda's cue. Usually, Laurette Taylor didn't hear it because she was drunk, and she was either asleep in the wings or fighting with the stage manager. So Laura had to yell it.'

'Did Laurette Taylor always hear her when she shouted it?'

'No, not always. If she didn't, Laura would limp back to the sideboard, pick up another little glass animal, limp all the way back across the stage to the Gentleman Caller and scream, "Here's another *SOUVENIR*!"'

Tennessee told us he gave half the royalties of the play to his mother. 'What did she do with the money?' I asked. He smiled sadly. 'She used it to divorce my father.'

The question I was most curious about was whether his mother realised that Amanda was based on her. 'After the first night in Chicago,' he said, 'I took my mother round backstage to meet Laurette. We went into her dressing room. Laurette was sitting at the mirror, putting grease on her face to remove the greasepaint. I introduced them. Laurette turned to face my mom and said, "Well, Mrs Williams, how did ya like yourself tonight?"'

'How did your mom respond?' I asked.

He shrugged. 'She had it coming,' he said.

* * *

It was time to do a new play. I decided on a farce by Royce Ryton called *The Unvarnished Truth*. It had a completely original premise: in the first scene, a playwright, the author of successful West End whodunnits, accidentally kills his wife after a violent argument about who loves the other more; in a panic he phones his agent before he phones the police. The agent arrives first and, as the playwright tells him what happened, he realises that the truth is less believable than a better story which he can easily make up. During the course of the play, as accidental deaths continue to pile up before our eyes, the playwright is forced to continue inventing cover stories that are much more believable than what we saw actually happening. It was one of the funniest plays I had ever read.

Tim Brooke-Taylor played the playwright and Graeme Garden was the police inspector. It turned out to be inspired casting. We had capacity audiences on tour because their series *The Goodies* was so popular, and they were inventive in the play. Graeme demonstrated a gift for physical comedy that I hadn't fully known about, and his performance included some spectacular stunts. The agent was played by the playwright, Royce Ryton, who was one of the strangest and sweetest men I have ever encountered: he had a loud screechy voice, and long red hennaed hair that stood up on end like a fright wig; he wore Elton John glasses, shiny sequined jackets, a ludicrously large crucifix around his neck made of old iron nails, and high-heeled shoes. That was *off*-stage. On stage I made him dress more or less like a normal person, but the prevailing climate of near-hysteria that enveloped him was perfectly in keeping for an agent who thinks that his most valuable client may go to prison for multiple murders that he didn't commit.

77. The audience will accept any premise.

Georges Feydeau, the greatest writer of farce in the history of the French theatre, said that an audience will accept any premise as a starting point of a play. If you want the play to depend upon a particular fact, or problem – for instance, that there is a cow on the roof – just *assert* that there is a cow on the roof. Don't attempt to explain how it got there.

Studio executives, who regard themselves as kings of logic because they are mainly lawyers or accountants by training, may demand a back-story that explains *how* the cow got on the roof. That way lies disaster. But remember:

78. If you start with an absurd premise, you must follow it through with total logic.

In *The Unvarnished Truth* and in *A Little Hotel on the Side*, the plot depended in large measure on the audience's acceptance of an absurd premise. In *A Little Hotel* the premise was that one of the characters stutters every time it rains, and therefore cannot complete his words or sentences. The actor playing the part wanted, as part of his homework, to visit a speech therapist to learn about stuttering. I asked him not to, because what he would learn from the speech therapist would be that nobody stutters because it rains. I wondered if the audience would accept this premise. They did, without question. And so did the critics.

Watch *Roxanne*, Steve Martin's wonderful film based on the play *Cyrano de Bergerac*. It has an absurd premise that the audience accepts without question. As does the original play.

79. When two characters should not meet, throw them together as soon as you can.

This is another of Feydeau's rules, which Royce understood instinctively.

Many writers and producers persist in imagining that there's something funny about a scene in which two characters who should not meet just miss each other. I've *never* seen that get a laugh. It is obviously a much better idea to throw them together, because one of them – or maybe both of them, depending on the plot – *will have to tell a lie*. Probably, if you're writing it well, multiple lies, because one lie will inevitably lead to others.

This is funny because the audience knows they are lying. It creates the possibility of endless confusion, miscommunication and therefore more lying and more complexity next time they meet, meaning further complex and unpredictable developments of the story. The plot will blossom.

80. Beware mistaken-identity plots.

This is a personal rule of mine. Mistaken identity is an overused device. And it always results in a predictable ending as the mistake is unravelled. It was used to great effect by Gogol in *The Government Inspector*, by Shakespeare in *Twelfth Night* and *The Comedy of Errors*, by Oliver Goldsmith in *She Stoops to Conquer*, by Ray Cooney and Tony Hilton in *One for the Pot*, and in all of Terence and Plautus. Gogol used it to illuminate character in a profound way, and as a satirical attack on politics and government. In Shakespeare's hands even the most obvious devices become magical, but few others (if any) have that gift. *One for the*

Pot was a new approach to mistaken identity, using tricks derived from illusionists, so that two, three and then four identical brothers were seen simultaneously on stage. Otherwise, mistaken identity works all right in parody and in Gilbert and Sullivan (most of which actually *is* parody), or with a wholly original twist (like the suspense film *North by Northwest*, in which Cary Grant is mistaken for someone who doesn't actually exist). But unless you have a brilliant new take on this device, try to avoid it.

* * *

Michael Codron came to see *The Unvarnished Truth* in Cambridge, and took it to the Phoenix Theatre in the West End. In spite of the funniest opening night that I can remember, the reviews were mixed and it looked as though we might not survive long. Then, on Sunday, Bernard Levin reviewed it – with such an understanding of Royce Ryton's extraordinary work and the art of farce that I'm going to quote him in full:

> What, after all, do we ask of farce? That it should point some noble moral, provide a healing catharsis, stretch us on the rack of pity for suffering mankind? By no means: we ask only that it shall make us laugh, and I, who could never laugh at Feydeau, Rix or Travers, laughed at *The Unvarnished Truth* until the flood of my tears drowned several usherettes, the box office manager and the theatre cat . . .
>
> I may not reveal by what logically insane way the plot proceeds, but I can at least draw attention to the curious fact that the eight characters who enter upon the stage

alternate men and women with absolute regularity; nor is this a coincidence.

For now the ramshackle tower of Pelions and Ossas,[17] from which all successful farce must be built, begins to grow. Absurdity is heaped upon absurdity, catastrophe upon disaster, until the very roof will not accommodate the resultant mountain of lunacy. Even when it falls over Mr Ryton has not yet finished, for he builds it effortlessly up again solely to add another storey to it.

The dialogue is not of the wittiest, but it has something of the same surreal flavour as the plot; Mr Ryton's imagination has quite slipped its moorings, and no idea is too mad to be successfully incorporated. The same goes for much of the acting, especially that of the author himself, who exhibits the haphazard intensity of a demented laser-beam, and of Graeme Garden, clutching his disappearing sanity around him like a bishop surprised in the bathroom by the cleaning-lady and trying to hide behind the loofah.

Not an identity is mistaken, not a wife is swapped, not a trouser falls. Yet I spent the final ten slapstick minutes screaming so loudly that I thought the cast would have to stop and wait till I got over it. They would be waiting still.

In my view, this is a perfect response to a play about death, and miraculously Levin describes and captures the experience of that opening night. We ran six months.

Royce died last year. His 'important' play, *Crown Mat-*

---

17 'Pelion and Ossa flourish side by side, / Together in immortal books enrolled' William Wordsworth.

rimonial, a conventional drama about the abdication of Edward VIII, was mentioned in all his obituaries. His masterpiece, *The Unvarnished Truth*, described as 'a murder comedy', which it wasn't, was essentially dismissed. 'Twas ever thus.

81. *Ars est celare artem* (The art is to conceal the art).

This is the motto of the Footlights Dramatic Club at Cambridge. It is true.

Comedy is best when it looks effortless and easy. The problem is that if it looks easy, people tend to think that it *is* easy, so comedies are seldom treated with the respect accorded to a so-called 'serious' film or play. Comedy is always needed and wanted; although comedies almost never win an Oscar for Best Picture, paradoxically everyone agrees that Oscar shows are best when hosted by a funny comedian. But:

82. If you conceal the art, you can't expect people to see the artistry.

It's a Catch-22.

* * *

About a year and a half after I accepted the Cambridge job, I began to feel like writing again, but I couldn't think of anything. I remembered Tony's suggestion and, though still far from enthusiastic about his notion, I phoned him. 'Do you remember you had an idea for a comedy about the civil service?'

'Yes.'

'Have you done anything about it?'

'No,' he said cheerfully. 'Are you interested now?'

When we met he reminded me of a forgotten incident that had occurred when he was Editor of *Tonight* and I was still at Cambridge. In 1962 the Shadow Cabinet's spokesman for Home Affairs was the Labour MP Frank Soskice. He had been a campaigner against capital punishment, which was finally abolished in 1969. At the time, there was a notorious case of a man hanged for a murder he didn't commit. His name was Timothy Evans. Ludovic Kennedy wrote a book about it called *Ten Rillington Place*. There was also a film, starring Richard Attenborough. Frank Soskice, with Ludovic and Sidney Silverman MP, started a petition to secure a posthumous pardon for Timothy Evans. In two years they collected two and a half million signatures, and it was handed in to the Home Secretary.

But there was a snag: it was now after the 1964 election, which Labour won. Frank Soskice himself had been appointed the Home Secretary. And when his own petition was handed in to him, he rejected it! As Will Rogers said:

83. There's no trick to being a humorist when you have the whole government working for you.

Tony and I didn't know each other then, but it struck us separately as one of the most darkly comic and strangest stories we had ever read.[18] I didn't give it any further thought, but Tony did, wondering what could change a man's opinions so completely that he would reject his own petition. A strange transformation comes over a person when he or she gets into

---

18 Exactly the same thing happened recently. Alan Johnson MP made an impassioned plea to the Home Office not to send an asylum seeker back to Cameroon, where he had been tortured. That was in 2007. In 2009 the Home Secretary rejected the plea. The Home Secretary was Alan Johnson.

office, a compelling need to suppress rights for which they have previously fought. He concluded that it had to be something to do with the civil service: there must be a difference between a minister's policy and the ministry's policy.

That is why every opposition party promises to create more freedom of information but no government ever does: the trick is to make the rules more restrictive under the guise of making them less so. Tony named this the Law of Inverse Relevance, which states that the less you are going to do about something the more you have to talk about it.

Until *Yes Minister*, all comedy shows that featured civil servants portrayed them as boring people who wore bowler hats and drank a lot of tea. Tony had served on the Committee on the Future of Broadcasting, chaired by Lord Annan. He drafted a part of the Annan Report, and after working with some senior civil servants he knew that the popular image of them was false. Tony is something of an Establishment figure, which I am not, but he also has the eye of an outsider.

84. It helps to be an outsider.

You can be from the wrong class, the wrong culture, the wrong ethnic background, the wrong religion, the wrong colour or the wrong sexual orientation. It all helps you to see the hypocrisy, the lies, the cheating and therefore the comedy.

For instance, many of America's most successful comedians in recent years – Jim Carrey, Dan Aykroyd, John Candy, Michael J. Fox, Phil Hartman, Mike Myers – are not American at all. They are Canadian.

Tony's mother was English through and through, and many people seem to think he's related to the political Jays (Douglas and Peter), but his father Ernest Jay was from an immigrant Jewish family, an actor whose most famous role was that of Dennis the Dachshund in *Larry the Lamb in Toytown* on the BBC Home Service. I loved listening to it when I was little. Tony, with one foot inside the Establishment and one foot outside, has always reflected both his parents. He is both a conservative and an iconoclast willing to make a joke about almost anything.

As for me, born and brought up in Bath, where there was no Jewish community, I was the only Jewish boy out of four hundred boys at Kingswood School, founded by John Wesley for the sons of Methodist ministers. If you want to create an outsider, that's a good way to go about it.

By the time Tony and I started work on our series, it was late 1977. Harold Wilson was out of office and Tony had been reading the diaries of our best source, Richard Crossman.[19] He died in 1974, leaving behind his three-volume *Diaries of a Cabinet Minister*, covering his time in government from 1964 to 1970, which were published despite monumental legal opposition from the government.

It was easy to see why such a battle had been fought. The diaries revealed that the civil service actually runs the country, and how it does it. On his first day in office, slightly daunted by the huge pile of letters in his in-tray, Crossman's Private Secretary tells him that if he doesn't want to reply to them himself, all he has to do is move them over to the out-tray and

---

19 Crossman was a brilliant man: the son of a judge, he attended Winchester College, studied Classics at New College, Oxford, receiving a Double First and becoming a Fellow in 1931. At the outbreak of World War II he joined the civil service. When elected as an MP, he was firmly on the left wing of the Parliamentary Labour Party, a prominent Bevanite. Wilson became Prime Minister in 1964 and appointed Crossman Minister of Housing and Local Government. In 1966 he became Lord President of the Council and Leader of the House of Commons, and he was Secretary of State for Health and Social Security from 1968 to 1970.

the civil service will take care of them. Indeed, on the very first page of the diaries his Private Secretary says 'Yes Minister' to him when he patently means 'No Minister.' Tony suggested that *Yes Minister* would be a good, ironic title for our show.

Our series didn't reveal anything that was not previously known to the three thousand civil servants in Whitehall and a few hundred ministers and ex-ministers, but it revealed plenty to the rest of the country. Crossman had made *Yes Minister* possible.

We decided to see if we could find a way to encapsulate this enormous subject into a series of half-hour situation comedies. Neither of us had been in government, but we each had a friend to consult as a starting point: Tony arranged for us to talk to Marcia Falkender, whom he met on the series *A Prime Minister on Prime Ministers*, twelve one-hour programmes in which David Frost interviewed Harold Wilson about twelve different PMs. Tony was the editor. My first helper was Nelson Polsby, Professor of Political Science and Head of the Institute of Governmental Affairs at Stanford University, California. An unlikely source, one might think, but he was at that time the Visiting Professor at the LSE,[20] and as a well-informed outsider and shrewd observer of the British political and government scene he was full of insight. He, in turn, introduced me to the man who became our other principal source, Bernard Donoughue (now Lord Donoughue).[21]

---

20 We made Jim Hacker a graduate of the LSE.

21 In *Downing Street Diary*, Bernard Donoughue quotes Sir John Hunt, Head of the Home Civil Service, talking about the Crossman diary: 'Hunt says it is appalling. Terrible attacks on all the Labour leaders, especially Callaghan, Castle, Soskice and HW [Harold Wilson] and named civil servants. Hunt said it would bring the whole system into disrepute and would certainly be disastrous for this government to have its members denigrated in this way. He says [Barbara] Castle is described as "a boring old bag".' It is clear why Richard Crossman's nickname was Double Crossman.

Lady Falkender, previously known as Marcia Williams before being ennobled, if that's the appropriate word, had been Wilson's Political Secretary since long before he became leader of the Labour Party after Hugh Gaitskell's death. Bernard Donoughue was then Chief Policy Adviser and Head of the Policy Unit at Number 10, under Prime Minister Jim Callaghan, and had held the same post in the Wilson government 1974–6. They were both particularly expert at political in-fighting within government, which is what much of *Yes Minister* was about. We never met them together, we never even told either of them that we consulted the other (though they probably guessed) because – having worked side by side for Harold Wilson at 10 Downing Street – they had a deep dislike and distrust of each other.[22]

Our first task was to reduce the scope of the drama while not losing the dramatic truth. We invented an 'umbrella' department, the Ministry of Administrative Affairs, so that the Minister could have the right to get involved in almost any matter involving administration or bureaucracy. Besides which, a ministry that administrates other administrators delighted us as a comically unnecessary layer of bureaucracy. The number of top civil servants in a department is actually outlined by Sir Humphrey to Jim in the pilot/first episode,

22 To anyone familiar with *Yes Minister* shows or books, *Downing Street Diary* frequently reveals what an extraordinary source Bernard Donoughue was. For instance, in volume 1, page 50: 'How to take over No. 10: Apparently last time in 1964 was very humiliating, with the civil servants treating the political team contemptuously, refusing to allow them into any rooms in No. 10. They snatched away [headed] writing paper to prevent them writing letters. And locked the door between the Cabinet Office and No. 10 to prevent any communication.' We used that locked door in one of the most popular episodes of *Yes Prime Minister*, 'The Key', and all the political manoeuvrings over the location of offices. Access to the PM is everything. Marcia told us that she chose for her office a room between the Cabinet Room and the Men's loo, so she could overhear what Cabinet ministers were saying as they went in and out of Cabinet to pee, out of the PM's earshot. The raw material for the series came from both of them, in equal measure.

which takes place shortly after he is appointed to his job as a government minister:

Sir Humphrey Briefly, sir, I am the Permanent Under-Secretary of State, known as the Permanent Secretary. Woolley here is your Principal Private Secretary. I, too, have a Principal Private Secretary and he is the Principal Private Secretary to the Permanent Secretary. Directly responsible to me are ten Deputy Secretaries, eighty-seven Under-Secretaries and two hundred and nineteen Assistant Secretaries. Directly responsible to the Principal Private Secretaries are plain Private Secretaries. The Prime Minister will be appointing two Parliamentary Under-Secretaries and you will be appointing your own Parliamentary Private Secretary.

Hacker *(joking)* Can they all type?

Sir Humphrey None of us can type, Minister. Mrs Mackay types. She is your secretary.

Obviously, all of these people could not be shown on a weekly basis.

85. Dramatic truth is not the same as real-life truth.

We felt that we could preserve the essential truth by narrowing it down to just three people, a dramatic triangle of the Minister, the Permanent Secretary and the Minister's Private Secretary, who hovers somewhere in between and has allegiance to both. 'When the chips are down, Bernard,' asks Hacker, 'whose side are you really on?' 'Minister,' replies Bernard with characteristic evasion and honesty, 'it's my job to see that the chips stay up.' Later, much later, we realised that we had stumbled onto a well-tried comic formula, the basis of Jeeves and Bertie Wooster, *The Admirable Crichton* and *The Servant of Two Masters*: the master who is less able than the servant.

We wrote a brief format and offered it to James Gilbert, Head of Comedy at BBC TV. The Minister was to be called Gerry Hacker. 'Hacker' didn't then have the internet computer connotations that it does today. I thought of Hacker simply because it evoked an image of a lost and desperate politician, blindly and hopelessly hacking his way through the undergrowth of the Whitehall jungle. I called the Civil Servant Humphrey after Humphrey Barclay, who was the most upper-class classicist I knew and seemed to me to have similar political skills. His surname, Appleby, came from nowhere, but it seemed suitably English and bucolic. 'Bernard Woolley' is self-explanatory. Tony didn't much mind what names we gave them.

Gilbert liked the idea and commissioned a pilot. We decided that the pilot should be about the fundamental issue: open government. Today's buzzword is 'transparency'. In Sir Humphrey's view, the words 'open government' are incompatible: you can be open, or you can have government. But Jim's party (it is never specified if it is Labour or Conservative) has just won an election, and one plank of its winning platform was open government. Humphrey has to find a way to nullify this pledge by exposing Jim to the dangers of too much openness.

86. The Hideous Dilemma frequently takes the form of Fear of Exposure – fear of other people knowing what you did or what you are really like.

This was not hard for Humphrey. There are many threats to a minister, but although they appear in a variety of guises they amount to only two: bad publicity followed by a fall in the opinion polls, and the fear of losing the job because you have lost the Prime Minister's favour. The former nearly always leads to the latter. There are two ways of losing your Cabinet post: the first is by being too unpopular, and the second is by being too popular. 'The Prime Minister giveth and the Prime Minister taketh away. Blessed be the name of the Prime Minister.' We established early on that whenever Sir Humphrey congratulated Jim for his bravery, Jim clearly understood that his job would be in jeopardy. 'Doing something controversial loses you votes,' explained Sir Arnold, the Cabinet Secretary and Sir Humphrey's boss, 'but doing something courageous can lose you the election.' Transparency about what is going on in government is, by definition, courageous.

It was some years later that we got official confirmation of this civil-service technique, when Sir Robert Armstrong, the Cabinet Secretary, admitted in a public inquiry that he had been 'economical with the truth', a marvellous euphemism truly in the style of Sir Humphrey, who had already opined: 'The citizens of a democracy have a right to be ignorant, and so do their elected representatives. Knowledge only means complicity and guilt. Ignorance has a certain dignity.' Hence Bush's and Blair's absurd attempts to make us think that they declared war on Iraq because of 'faulty intelligence'.

Our elected leaders, the programme said, do not suppress the facts. They merely take a democratic decision not to publish them. This, of course, is done only from the best motives, for reasons of security, and is a time-honoured government procedure. In the words of Sir Francis Bacon, the Elizabethan poet, philosopher and civil servant: 'He that would keep a secret must keep it secret that he hath a secret to keep.' The guiding principle that overtakes all governments is this: 'If nobody knows what you are doing, then nobody knows what you are doing wrong.'

We wrote 'Open Government'. John Howard Davies was now Head of Comedy, and he liked it. We met to discuss casting. Tony and I wanted Paul Eddington as Gerry Hacker and Nigel Hawthorne as Sir Humphrey. We each think we suggested him first. We had both seen Nigel on stage in *Privates on Parade* and *Otherwise Engaged*, and as Sir Walter Monckton in a series about the abdication of Edward VIII, and felt that he was the perfect actor for the part. I had seen Paul at the Bristol Old Vic in *The Apple Cart* when I was a teenager, and then in *The Tenth Man* and numerous other West End plays. Tony loved him in *The Good Life*, in which I had played a guest part for one week and got to know him a little. We opened the meeting by suggesting Paul for Hacker. John promptly agreed. Then he suggested Nigel for Sir Humphrey. We promptly agreed. The meeting was over. It was the easiest casting session in my career.

Now we actually had to get them. First we changed Gerry Hacker's name to Jim, because John reminded us that Paul's character in *The Good Life* was called Gerry. The script was sent to them. They both liked it, but both sensibly said that they weren't willing to commit to a series on the basis of one good script. They had to see more and know how it developed. The unspoken question was: 'How do we know that Tony and Jonathan can write more than one script of this quality?' It was a fair question, and the BBC commissioned another script. We wrote it, they liked it, but asked to see more. In this fashion we wrote the first four scripts. After they read the fourth and said they still needed to see more, Tony and I drew the line. No, we said, four scripts are enough, they must make up their minds, yes or no. They agreed to do the pilot.

However, before signing up, Paul phoned me. I didn't know him well. He told me that he would rather play Sir Humphrey. I had to talk him out of this as we had already cast Nigel, and Tony and I both thought he would be the perfect Jim. I succeeded by pointing out that, as the Minister, he had the title role. As the years went by he referred to this conversation with increasing bitterness because Sir Humphrey had turned out to be the best part, as he had suspected. Nigel eventually won four BAFTA Awards for Best Actor in a Situation Comedy. Paul, though nominated as many times as Nigel, never won. This was a great injustice because Paul was superb as Jim Hacker; but, as every actor knows, without the role you can't win the prize. Sometimes the role wins the prize for you.

Casting Bernard Woolley was much more difficult. Initially I wondered if I should play him, but I decided to put my Cambridge Theatre Company commitments first. In retrospect, this seems like a foolish decision, but I had not done the best job I could when acting in my own scripts of *My Brother's Keeper* and I decided to focus on the writing, not a full-time job as there were only three more episodes to write. The part was turned down by a number of actors who didn't think the part was good enough. This is a common phenomenon: all the 'big name' Italian-American actresses in the US declined the part of Lisa in *My Cousin Vinny* because 'the part isn't good enough'; I cast a virtual unknown, Marisa Tomei, and she won the Oscar. Keep in mind:

87. Just because lots of agents and actors reject a part as 'not good enough', that doesn't mean it's not good enough.

I found myself at a dinner party one night at Holloway Prison, with the Governor and his wife, and Derek Fowlds. His open, amiable manner is extremely attractive to audiences. I suggested him the next day, and we had our Bernard. He liked the part: he could read.

Eventually it was time to shoot the pilot. The BBC engaged the producer/director of *On the Buses* to direct it. This worried me. All went well at the read-through on the Monday, the first blocking day, and I returned without Tony, who was busy at Video Arts, to see the rehearsal on Wednesday. I was shocked. The script had been rewritten. Paul was now playing a new, silly and bad 'sitcom' scene in which he was fussing around choosing fabric for his office sofa. At the end of the scene they looked at me for approval. Regretting that Tony wasn't there to support me, but fairly certain that he would agree, I didn't mince words. I said that what I had seen was not acceptable and it had to be played as we wrote it.

'But this new stuff is funny,' said the director.

'Not in my opinion,' I said. 'It trivialises the whole show. This is not what Jim Hacker is going to be concerned about on his first day in office. The scene was much better and funnier the way we wrote it.'

The director looked at me with scepticism. 'It's *clever*,' he said with condescension. (It's interesting how often the

English use 'clever' as a term of disparagement. Hence the insult 'too clever by half'.) 'It's very *clever*. But we have an audience coming in on Sunday. We need to get some laughs.'

'This will get laughs if you play it as written,' I insisted, though with more hope than certainty.

'Not very many,' he said.

'I don't agree,' I said. My heart was pounding but I stayed outwardly calm. 'Look, this is the script that the BBC bought, that Paul and Nigel signed on for, and that you agreed to direct. We don't agree to your changing it. If you do, the show won't happen on Sunday night. Tony and I will see that it's stopped. We'll call our agents today. There will be no show.' I had no idea of my contractual position, nor did I have any reason to suppose that I had a legal leg to stand on. I was bluffing.

There was a bit of a pause after I uttered this threat. Then Paul said: 'I think, you know, if Jonathan feels that strongly, we should try it his way.' Nigel agreed. They started rehearsing the scene again, as it was written. I didn't leave until they had it roughly right. The director wasn't happy. I immediately phoned Tony, who, as I'd hoped, reassured me that I'd done the right thing.

88. Never give an ultimatum unless you are prepared to stick to it.

This is a good rule for every aspect of your life.

Why did I take that risk in this case? I had been persuaded, or had persuaded myself (I don't know which), into betraying the original notion of *My Brother's Keeper*, and I learned from the experience. I had given up writing situation comedy once already, and I had no intention of going back to the same old thing. I really didn't want to do *Yes Minister* unless it was going to be different. It was not that Tony and I had any long-term expectations for it; on the contrary, the best we hoped for was to get six or seven programmes on the air for BBC2. Perhaps it was because of our low expectations that we weren't willing to compromise, nor to talk down to the audience. Tony liked to quote C. P. Scott, the first editor of the *Manchester Guardian*: 'Never underestimate the intelligence of the reader, but never overestimate his information.'[23]

89. If the necessary information is contained in a script, the viewer will be intelligent enough to understand the abbreviations or the jargon.

That Sunday we recorded the show. I had asserted, with a confidence that I did not wholly feel, that it would get laughs. Neither of us quite expected the gales of laughter that came from the studio audience that night. John Howard Davies lost little time in commissioning three more scripts, to make the first series of seven. Then we waited, and waited ... and waited.

The Winter of Discontent approached and government all but broke down, and the BBC refused to transmit the first series until after the forthcoming election, which turned out to be not until 1979. They were scared that it would be seen as improperly influencing the election. Finally, three years after we had first proposed the show to the BBC, we went on the air in February 1980.

---

23 For instance, the first time the MoD or GNP were mentioned in an episode, they would be called the Ministry of Defence or the Gross National Product. Not thereafter.

Throughout the run of the series most people assumed that we were writing about the Thatcher government. She was indeed the Prime Minister during the whole time that the series were on the air, but we wrote the first series when Jim Callaghan was Prime Minister and the Labour Party was in power. In that series Jim Hacker had a Special Political Adviser called Frank Wiesel (he pronounced it 'Wy-sel', though everyone else called him Weasel), who was clearly a Labour man. On the whole, Conservatives didn't have advisers of this sort, and we wrote him out after the first series, to seem more current.

The series eventually ran from 1980 to 1988 but was not about the eighties. It was devised in the seventies and reflected the media-obsessed politics of the Wilson/Heath/Callaghan years, not the conviction politics of Margaret Thatcher. It was actually much closer to the politics of the years that followed, the years of Major, Blair and Brown. In any case, there is a timelessness about good comedy: the pleasure and excitement of recognition are not rooted in a particular time or place. Humanity remains constant.

* * *

Throughout the ten years we wrote together Tony only worked between nine and five, from Monday to Friday. He is a very organised man. As chairman and chief writer of Video Arts he already had a busy life. I was just as occupied directing at the CTC, then in the West End, the RSC and the NT. Although we decided to find the time to dovetail the writing into our other work, this did not include evenings or weekends, which were sacrosanct to Tony. As an actor and director, used to working all hours, I found this rather a startling notion. Cleese remarked to me: 'Life has most people by the throat. Tony has life by the throat.'

For each series we would set a schedule. There was little leeway. We allowed up to two weeks for constructing a story, and no more than five mornings for actually writing the script. Usually it took only four mornings because, once we had the plot and a scene breakdown and we knew exactly who needed what from whom and who had leverage over whom, the dialogue came relatively easily.

90. Plan your time. Exercise self-discipline. When it is time to write, write.

On writing days we would start between 8.30 and 9am. If Tony had a lunch for Video Arts business, we would write until noon. If I was rehearsing a play, we stopped at 11.15am, leaving me forty-five minutes to get across London, in time for rehearsal between noon and 6pm. If I was not rehearsing and Tony had no business lunch, we would work until 12.30 or even – occasionally – one o'clock, but never in the afternoon. For Tony, afternoons were *Yes Minister*-free zones. They were for Video Arts, sitting in his garden or napping.

91. Get something – anything – down on paper (or on your computer). Rewriting and editing are easier than writing.

My partnership with Tony is the best working relationship I have ever had. In those ten years we never had a row. Occasional disagreements about the scripts, of course, but from the outset we implicitly granted each other the right of veto.

If either of us felt strongly enough about anything, either for or against, the other would acquiesce.

We were totally patient with each other's foibles. We never had an accounting for drinks, lunches and so forth; if we had, I would now owe Tony a lot of money. But there was one sort of debt that we both rigorously enforced: I lived in Hampstead Garden Suburb, Tony lived in Ealing, and we were connected and separated by the North Circular Road, which was being reconstructed for virtually the entire time we worked together. In the rush hour it was a ten-mile-long car park. We took turns to write at each other's house and the drive could take up to an hour each way, sometimes more if there was an event at Wembley. We kept the strictest record of whose turn it was to brave the traffic, and there was no quarter asked or given on this matter. Driving debts had to be repaid.

Tony often says that he learned how to write comedy from me, but I don't think that could be true, for he is a very funny man and he was an experienced writer. I do know that I learned from him how the world works. I learned a little detachment too, though that's never been my strong suit and still isn't. Tony has observed that he was the guardian of Sir Humphrey's soul and I was the guardian of Jim Hacker's, and, although we wrote both characters together, there is truth in this. Tony, like Sir Humphrey, has a First in Classics, is fluent in Latin and Greek and has an academic, analytical mind. He would probably have become a Permanent Secretary had he joined the civil service instead of the BBC.

Occasionally, he was unconsciously funny. One day, when we were writing and discussing the national integrated transport policy that we were inventing, Jim Hacker commented that if there were votes in the policy he certainly didn't want to look a gift horse in the mouth. Tony wrote this line for

Humphrey: 'I put it to you, Minister, that you are looking a *Trojan* horse in the mouth.'

I then wrote a line for Hacker: 'You mean, if we look closely at this gift horse we'll find it's full of Trojans?'

I passed the sheet of paper across the desk to Tony. 'Well, no,' he said. 'If one had looked the Trojan horse in the mouth one would have found Greeks inside, because the Greeks gave the horse to the Trojans. So technically it wasn't a Trojan horse at all, it was a Greek horse. Hence the tag *Timeo Danaos et dona ferentes*, which is usually and somewhat inaccurately translated as "Beware of Greeks bearing gifts."'

I foolishly asked him what a better translation of that Greek tag would be.

'No,' said Tony patiently, 'it's a Latin tag. It's obvious really, the Greeks would hardly have advised other people to beware of Greeks. But there's another way you can tell: the tag is clearly Latin rather than Greek, not because *timeo* ends in "o", because the Greek first person also ends in "o" – actually there is a Greek word *timao* meaning "I honour" – but because the "os" ending is a nominative singular termination of the second declension in Greek and an accusative plural in Latin. Incidentally, *Danaos* is not only the Greek for Greek but the Latin for Greek too.'

As he spoke I realised that it was all perfectly in character for Bernard, and I hurriedly scribbled down everything he was saying and popped it into the script. It got big laughs and Tony was benignly pleased that his arcane academic knowledge struck other people as amusing.

92. Don't use puns, except to illuminate character.

The purpose of a pun is to excite admiration for the punster's wit. So, although they may be entertaining in conversation or in a certain style of prose, they are a literary device that is seldom of any use in dialogue form. They are too artificial and self-conscious. However, they are useful in creating a comically irritating or pedantic character, such as Bernard Woolley in *Yes Minister*, a man who is obsessed – to a fault – with language.

93. Be brief, usually.

Witty and funny lines should be brief and to the point. But there are exceptions to this, because not all comedy comes from wit. Even though the writer is witty, the characters may not be. Like Bernard and Sir Humphrey (or like Polonius, who originally said that brevity is the soul of wit in the course of an immensely long and comically tedious speech), they may be funny because of their pedantry and verbosity:

Sir Humphrey It's clear that the committee has agreed that your new policy is really an excellent plan but in view of some of the doubts being expressed, may I propose that I recall that, after careful consideration, the considered view of the committee was that while they considered that the proposal met with broad approval in principle, that some of the principles were sufficiently fundamental in principle and some of the considerations so complex and finely balanced in practice that, in principle, it was proposed that the sensible and prudent practice would be to submit the proposal for more detailed consideration, laying stress on the essential continuity of the new proposal with existing principles, and the principle of the principal arguments which the proposal proposes and propounds for their approval, in principle.

Just as Tony has much in common with Sir Humphrey, I am not unlike Jim Hacker, a frustrated and disappointed idealist who regularly fails to practise what he preaches. I think that most politicians set out to do some good, but as they climb higher and higher up the greasy pole they are forced to accept one compromise after another until finally they have lost their souls. They lose sight of the reasons why they went into politics to start with. Staying in office becomes the whole objective. They see no contradiction in this: after all, how can they do any good if they are out of office? So they will swallow anything in order to stay in power. They are like Graham Greene's whisky priest. Even though they mostly end up as unprincipled hypocrites, I'm sorry for them. And sorrier for the rest of us.

We expected that the show would be derided by politicians and civil servants alike. But we had portrayed civil servants as politicians saw them, and politicians as civil servants saw them. Because both sides loved enough of it, it was not thought of as mean-spirited or cruel. In this we were greatly aided by the immense charm of the actors, who made likeable the reprehensible characters they were playing.

People always ask song-writing teams: Which comes first, the music or the lyrics? I am always asked: How do you write with someone else?

94. Writing with someone else is easy if you leave your ego out of it.

I was always grateful if Tony came up with a better idea or

line, and so was he when I did. It makes the whole process faster and easier. A half-formed idea is useless if you're by yourself, but it may open a door to a line of dialogue or to a whole story if you have a writing partner who can run with it. I found the same when I wrote with George.

95. Every collaboration is different. It depends on the collaborators.

All writing teams are different. Keith Waterhouse and Willis Hall sometimes used to write whole episodes of their series separately. Bill Oddie and Graeme Garden, writing the *Doctor* shows, each wrote half an episode. Hanging out, I watched a couple of Cleese–Chapman writing sessions, which were extraordinary. John would sit at the typewriter, painstakingly writing and questioning every tiny detail down to the punctuation, while Graham, who usually arrived hungover an hour or so late, would lie on the floor, read *Playboy* and occasionally bark at the ceiling. I asked John whether he thought it was fair that he did all the work. 'Yes,' he said, 'because about once every two days Graham comes up with an idea that is so funny that it makes it all worth it.'

Tony and I always wrote together, sitting opposite each other. We would talk through a story in general terms, then in greater and greater detail until we knew what each scene had to contain. Then, finally, whichever of us had less inertia that morning would pick up a pen and start writing. If we got stuck we would simply pass the pad of paper to the other. If one of us were on a roll we would finish a whole page or even a whole scene, then give it to the other – who would make small changes, or cuts, or write in additions. Sometimes one of us would decide that the other was barking up the wrong tree and completely redraft the scene. There were no rules, and there were no hurt feelings. Mostly, by the time the script was completed we genuinely didn't know who had written what, and we didn't care.

Our other jobs meant that, as we wrote for very few hours a day, a series took quite a long time to complete. Sometimes we would write two episodes back to back, for which we would allow five to six weeks of morning sessions (three hours each). There would normally be a gap of several weeks before we could resume. A series might typically be written over a nine-month period. This gave us a lot of time for reflection. We never wrote while a series was in production: we would complete an entire series and then, about six weeks before filming and recording started, we would have a read-through with the principal cast of all the scripts, over about two days. This was the actors' opportunity to suggest anything to us, and for us to see where improvements were still needed.

96. Know your actors, and accommodate them where possible.

By the first day of rehearsal the scripts were almost set in stone, and only minute changes were made after that. Indeed, Nigel, who was adamant that he would never use an autocue nor have any cribs on his desk, had so many long and difficult speeches to learn that he soon made us promise not to change any of his lines within three weeks of starting to rehearse an episode. For him to be in character, he had to know the lines. Paul, a more practical man, had no such worries and his desk and other items of furniture around the set had crib sheets everywhere amongst the official papers.

Early on in the first series Paul came to a line, stopped, didn't say it but asked: 'Can I just *act* this?' 'Show us,' we said. He did, and the meaning was clear and was funny. From then on there were usually a couple of lines for Paul in each script that were followed by the stage direction: PAUL NEEDN'T SAY THIS. HE CAN ACT IT IF HE PREFERS. We always wrote the dialogue, however, to be sure that he knew *what* he was supposed to be acting.

Paul had always been politically aware. He was a Quaker and had been a conscientious objector during World War II. He rapidly became interested in the subject matter of the series, and would arrive at rehearsal gleefully brandishing the *Guardian*, reading out government statements with relish and then interpreting them, reading between the lines for the real meaning.

Nigel, a South African and a refugee from the apartheid regime, was undoubtedly left of centre but in a generalised, emotional sort of way. 'I'm not interested in politics. Never have been,' he confided to me on several occasions. As a result, though he understood Sir Humphrey, he never really grasped the wider context of the show. When we explained things to Paul that he hadn't understood in the script, we gave them a political context. That didn't work with Nigel. Tony hit upon a better way fairly early on, when Nigel took us aside after a read-through on the first day of a show and said that he just couldn't see why Humphrey was behaving like this. 'Well,' said Tony, 'he's like Malvolio this week.' 'Ah!' said Nigel, as a great light dawned. That was the help he needed. Another week Tony said: 'This week it's Iago,' and Nigel was off and running.

97. Topicality doesn't matter. Human nature doesn't change.

We are often asked how the programmes seem relevant and even topical more than twenty years later. The reason is that the topicality was an illusion. A few of the shows were topical when they were written, because our sources had let us know of hidden crises or agenda that might come to the boil in the next few months. Mostly, however, as the shows were written up to a year in advance of transmission, the effect was created by popping in a topical line or two on the week that we did the show.

In fact, even that wasn't necessary. In August 1986, when we started out on *Yes Prime Minister*, we looked at the main stories in the *Daily Telegraph* for the same month, thirty years earlier: August 1956. The stories were all the same as today: Should we or shouldn't we be in Europe? Why don't we trust the French, or like the Germans (or vice versa)? Is the Franco-German alliance dominating Europe at our expense? Why should we give so much money to the Common Agricultural Policy, just to support French farmers? How will Europe affect our special relationship with America? What do we do about an impending war in the Middle East? What about the environment? Is there a risk of inflation/deflation (delete where not applicable)? Is the NHS getting even worse and are the waiting lists getting longer? Why are house prices rising again? What's wrong with the Honours list? How do we get defence spending under control? Why don't we have a national transport policy?

There were stories about party conferences, leak inquiries, leadership challenges and repelling boarders. Nothing was different, except for the names and the inflated numbers. The stories were unchanged, fifty years later. They remain the same today.

With the stage play *Yes Prime Minister*, written twenty-three years later, we found yet again that what we wrote in 2009 was topical in 2010 when we opened at Chichester, seemingly even more topical when it transferred to the Gielgud Theatre on Shaftesbury Avenue four months later, and bang up to the minute when it went on tour in the spring of 2011. Only two or three lines were updated in that period.

* * *

We would start out on a series with about three weeks' worth of lunches and meetings with sources who wanted to remain anonymous. We had mapped out in advance rough political areas that interested us and which seemed comically fruitful due to one form of hypocrisy or another. We had lunches and further meetings with Marcia and Bernard, to test our initial thoughts. Then we went off to start roughing out stories. Gradually we would find experts in the field of each story to check it out, *before* it was written. These other sources were a variety of people: ex-ministers of both parties, political journalists who wrote about the topic, and – when lucky – current ministers.

The lower down the hierarchy politicians were, the less use they were to us, but not for the reason one might have imagined: it wasn't only that they knew less, they were cowed by the Official Secrets Act. As the old joke says, the Official Secrets Act is not there to protect secrets but to protect officials. High up the food chain, politicians are much less careful. In fact, it was pretty much a rule of thumb that the higher up they are, the more indiscreet they will be. After all, leaking is an indispensable tool of government. Politicians may not be more sinned against than sinning, but apart from Tony Blair they are more leaked against than leaking.

They all do it. Senior politicians always have an axe to grind, a point of view that they want aired or tested, and once they realised that we were not going to name our sources we found that if we gave a politician lunch with a bottle or two of good claret they would tell us everything we needed to know. We never wasted time talking to backbench MPs unless they had been government ministers, and we never wrote a scene in the chamber of the House of Commons because government does not take place there. The House of Commons is theatre. That's where the performance takes place. Decisions are taken elsewhere.

We also had some useful sources among civil servants. Current civil servants were intentionally helpful only when authorised. Robin Butler, Mrs Thatcher's Private Secretary,[24] was extremely kind, and he showed us all around 10 Downing Street and answered a lot of non-controversial questions, but only because she had told him to and Bernard Donoughue had told him that we could be trusted. We had access to all the rooms in the building that were seen in any episode of *Yes Prime Minister*, but in return we promised to change the internal geography of the house on screen, for security reasons. Of course, we were happy to comply with that request.

One or two civil servants were unintentionally helpful. We had a long talk with a current Permanent Secretary before we began writing the second series. He was welcoming and

---

24 Later (like Sir Humphrey) Cabinet Secretary and Head of the Civil Service. Now Lord Butler.

friendly, apparently subscribing to Sir Humphrey's adage, 'Always tell the press and the public, frankly and openly, anything that they can easily find out some other way.'

He had enjoyed the first series, and Tony began our meeting by asking him what, if anything, we had got wrong. People love to answer that question. Everybody likes being an expert. He said: 'I thought it was really very good, very funny. But since you're asking, there was one thing . . .'

'What was that?' we asked.

'In one episode you suggested a situation in which a civil servant might do the wrong thing if promised an honour of some sort. That was really rather a frightful blemish.'

A wonderful hint! The very next morning we started investigating the honours list and it soon became clear that, when it came to honours, the civil service had plenty to be embarrassed about.[25]

* * *

The night that the first episode was broadcast we got mixed reviews. Immediately after the first show went on the air there was a radio interview on *Kaleidoscope*, a Radio 4 arts programme, with Sir Richard Marsh, then regarded as an expert on everything in government despite having been Chairman of British Rail, which was one of the biggest jokes in Britain.[26] He told the listeners that we'd got it all wrong and was thoroughly condescending.

TV professionals whom we met loved it. Humphrey Barclay phoned me immediately after the first show, full of

---

25 See Chapter Ten of *The Complete Yes Minister*.
26 And an ex-Minister of Transport. Shortly after his review was broadcast he was elevated to Lord Marsh and kicked upstairs from the animals to the vegetables.

enthusiasm, certain that it would be a hit. Denis Norden said the same to Tony. No one took much notice of the second episode, but everything changed after the third week. This sudden surge of enthusiasm was the result of a lengthy article by Roy Hattersley in the *Spectator*. Hattersley was Deputy Leader of the Labour Party at the time and, like Jim Prior in the Tory Party and Jim Hacker in our series, was a centrist politician who could have belonged to either party. Hattersley described everything that the show had shown so far, confirmed that this was exactly what had happened to him when he first became a minister, and asked how on earth did we know?

Hattersley's article galvanised the political press. Suddenly political correspondents took up the show and editorials started to be written about it. The TV critics, late to the party, jumped on the bandwagon, and after the fourth episode the critic from the *Evening Standard* told his readers that *Yes Minister* was an excellent comedy show and he had said so from the start. He hadn't.

98. Beware a phone call from the Inland Revenue, even if it's an invitation to lunch.

Perhaps stimulated by the Hattersley piece, other unlikely people suddenly showed an interest. Almost immediately after Episode Three and the *Spectator* article, we were phoned by Sir Lawrence Airey, Chairman of the Inland Revenue. He explained that although he was not called Permanent Secretary to the Inland Revenue, that was in fact his rank. He told us how much he liked the three programmes he had seen and invited us to lunch. Gratified, we accepted. It was to be our first meeting with a current Permanent Secretary.

We had been expecting to meet at a discreet little restaurant and we were disconcerted when lunch turned out to be at the headquarters of the Revenue, Somerset House, beside Waterloo Bridge. When we arrived we were admitted by uniformed men with large jangling key rings with lots of keys, rather like a prison. Entering through heavy gates made of black steel bars, we followed the warders along vast cavernous corridors until we reached more locked gates. At every gate we stepped through and waited, while the guards locked them behind us. Eventually, up some stairs, we reached the boardroom, and there waiting for us was the entire Board of the Inland Revenue, all eleven members.

We accepted an offer of sherry, and a thimbleful came our way. Lunch was like being back at school, a dull selection of tasteless cold cuts with lettuce and cucumber and tomatoes and Heinz Salad Dressing. The Board members were a chilly crowd, but did their best to appear amiable, and Sir Lawrence led the conversation. There were many compliments from the good cops in the room, but many more questions about where we were getting our information. We ducked them all as politely as we could, having made promises of anonymity to our various sources.

We left after what had seemed a very long hour and three-quarters, with Sir Lawrence muttering confidentially as we shook hands, 'Let me know what you hear. I'd love to help, I can tell you if what you're hearing is right or wrong.' It seemed an uncharacteristically cooperative attitude, coming from a Permanent Secretary. We didn't say much to each other until we had completed the long, echoing march back to the main gate and were back out in the car park. I felt I'd served eighteen months.

We were puzzled by the meeting, but not for long: at 3pm that day we were due to meet Marcia Williams at her little mews house off Baker Street. We started to tell her about lunch, and she immediately interrupted us: 'Oh no. Tell me you didn't go to lunch at the Revenue.'

We admitted that we had. 'Oh God!' she said. 'You didn't fall for that?' Shamed by our naivety, we asked what exactly we had fallen for. 'What did you tell them?' she asked. We summarised the conversation. She smiled a bleak smile.

'What's the problem?' I said.

'The Revenue is Whitehall's police force. Didn't you know? They were trying to find out what you know and where you're getting your information.'

'He was quite helpful,' I said. 'He offered to check our information out for us.'

'Of course he did. Then he'd know where you were getting it.'

'We didn't tell him anything,' Tony said firmly. 'I'm sure they could see that we're no threat to national security. They were probably trying to discover if we are just a couple of harmless funny people or seriously subversive.'

'Seriously subversive?' I remarked. 'That's ridiculous! We went to Cambridge.'

'As did Philby, Burgess and Maclean,' said Marcia.

'Why does the Revenue function as Whitehall's police force?' I asked.

'It's because they have so much information about everyone. They know everything about you and everyone: how much you earn, how much you spend, what you spend it on, where you go, what you do – they can work most of it out from the receipts. And they have the most comprehensive press-clipping service in the country.'

'What for?'

Marcia role-played a tax inspector. 'Mr Lynn, look at this clipping. This *is* you in this photograph, isn't it? It shows you outside Tramps, getting into a chauffeur-driven Rolls-Royce. Look, here's another picture: there you are, driving a Porsche. And here you are at the Cannes Film Festival, drinking the finest champagne – four bottles of Dom, according to your receipt which I have here. And look, here's a photo of you coming out of the Hotel du Cap. Tell me, Mr Lynn, how do you do all this on fifty-one thousand a year?'

We didn't hear from Sir Lawrence Airey, and although I dismissed this conversation with Marcia as paranoia, we didn't consult him on the next script. Then, a few weeks after our lunch at Somerset House, I was audited by the Revenue. Their investigation took three years. Many people whom I knew in television had dubious offshore companies in the Channel Islands that were later successfully challenged in court and, years after the money was all spent, they were suddenly faced with gigantic bills for back taxes. I was glad that I had not been tempted by the many people who had said to me, 'Why don't you meet my accountant? I don't pay any tax at all.' If something sounds too good to be true, it usually is, and I had trodden the straight and narrow. For three years the Revenue investigated me and at the end of it all it was a draw: I owed them a little money, but they owed me approximately the same amount.

It would have been disastrous for the credibility of *Yes Minister* if I had been fiddling my taxes. Whether it was a fishing expedition, an attempt to intimidate me or just a co-incidence, I shall never know. But every December, including the three years I was being audited, I received a card from Sir Lawrence Airey and the Board of the Inland Revenue wishing me a Merry Christmas and a Happy New Year.

The Inland Revenue as Whitehall's police force would have been an excellent subject for a *Yes Minister* script, but we never wrote one. It seemed that it might be unwise.

99. Truth is often funnier than fiction.

We realised that, just like the Video Arts films, *Yes Minister* was a series of training films for members of the government, showing them how not to do it. The more detailed, accurate and thorough our research, the funnier our scripts became. The driest government reports became unexpected sources of hilarity and wonder. For instance, the Fulton Report into the Civil Service (1968) revealed the number of accountants employed at the Treasury. How many would you expect? Two hundred? Three hundred? Two thousand? In fact, when the report was written there were no accountants at the Treasury. Economists? Plenty. Statisticians? Certainly. Accountants? None at all.

So we rang the Treasury and spoke to the Press Office. 'Have any accountants been taken on since the Fulton Report, or are there still none?'

'Oh no, it's quite different now,' the Press Officer replied.

'So how many are there?'

'Well,' he said carefully, 'I'm sure there's at least one.'

We asked him to check up. He rang back half an hour later, triumphant. 'I was completely wrong,' he said. 'There are, in fact, three or four accountants working at the Treasury.'

I wanted to be sure that the number was so small. 'Four?' I

said, giving them the benefit of the doubt. 'Four full-time accountants?'

'Wait a minute,' he said, careful again. 'I didn't say that they're full-time *or* that they're employed by the Treasury.' I waited. 'They are actually part-time and they're on secondment from other government departments.' No wonder our tax forms are so hard to complete.

We could never have made that up. Nor could we have made up the fact that the Foreign Secretary got his foreign news from watching TV but, in those days before the internet, he did. Of course, the Foreign Office cables eventually arrived, a couple of days later, with somewhat fuller information than you got from ITN, but if there was a *coup d'état*, or a diplomatic kidnapping or hijacking, the Foreign Secretary learned it from the telly just like the rest of us.

We invented a scene in which about ten people piled into Jim Hacker's first-class railway sleeping compartment to discuss a sudden crisis. An identically ridiculous scene took place in Harold Wilson's sleeper when he was Prime Minister, on the way to a party conference in Blackpool. We wrote an incident in which the leader of a small African country chartered a jumbo-jet, which was referred to by the patronising Sir Humphrey as 'the mumbo-jumbo', and painted a fictitious logo on the side so as to make people think that this little country had a national airline. Many countries invented fictional airlines, whenever the UN General Assembly met. A national airline was an important status symbol.

We did invent, for the National Health Service, the ultimate absurdity: an empty hospital with its full quota of five hundred administrative staff and auxiliary workers but with no medical staff and no patients. We gave it the 'Florence Nightingale Prize', awarded to the most hygienic hospital in the region. Then we discovered that there were, in fact, five or six such hospitals, or wings of hospitals, in the UK. One of them had just one patient: Matron, who had tripped over some scaffolding and broken her leg. We were learning to think like the civil service. And in our NHS researches we found some wonderful real-life memos, of which my favourite was 'Good Friday this year will be held on Tuesday April 13th.'

By the time the first seven episodes had been shown awards started coming our way. Not *our* way, actually, because the writers of a successful TV show are virtually invisible. When the BAFTA Awards came around, *Yes Minister* was nominated for Best Comedy Series. Nigel and Paul were both nominated for Best Actor in a Comedy Series. Nigel won Best Actor for Sir Humphrey. Producer Sydney Lotterby, who was brought in after we replaced the producer/ director of the pilot, won the Award for Best Comedy Series. Tony and I were not invited. Nigel and his partner Trevor, Paul and his wife Trish, Derek Fowlds and Sydney were all there, but not us. We won, but we watched it on TV at home.

I was annoyed and rightly so (as opposed to numerous other occasions in my life when I have been annoyed and wrongly so). Tony was irritated too but, phlegmatic as always, he chose to look at it historically: a group of film and TV technicians formed BAFTA to give themselves awards, but nobody was interested. So they added awards for actors, and suddenly everyone was interested. Writers, however, being mere 'schmucks with Underwoods',[27] did not bring any

---

27 Reputedly said by Jack L. Warner, the least appealing of these unappealing Bros.

publicity or glamour to the proceedings, so they didn't need to be included. Eventually, under pressure, BAFTA instituted The Writer's Award for Television.[28] In other words, BAFTA gave one writing award each year, covering all TV categories.

That was the history. Television writers at that time, especially 'comedy writers', were not accorded much respect. They were not, somehow, 'legit'. They were admired for being funny, and for their prolific output, but unless they wrote satire there were no accolades or even acknowledgements beyond the bare minimum. I think that the BBC's attitude to writers was, in some measure, responsible for this condescending imbalance.

I don't think that Tony or I were ever thanked by name on the three occasions that we won Best Situation Comedy for our producers. Even Nigel only referred to us as 'the writers' on the four occasions that he won the BAFTA Award for playing Sir Humphrey. Playwrights get thanked by name, but we were the backroom boys, the staff, people who wrote good jokes.

100. Virtually all comedy is situation comedy.

Situation comedy is not a subgenre of comedy. All dramatised comedy is situation comedy, or should be. Comedy comes from both character and plot (see Rule 103), which together create the situation. Good dialogue and/or physical comedy are the icing on the cake. The cake is the situation.

There are so many bad and mediocre 'sitcoms' that the phrase has become a pejorative shorthand, but among situ-

28 Now renamed the Dennis Potter Award.

ation comedies can be found some of the finest comedy writing of our time: in Britain, *Steptoe and Son*, *Dad's Army*, *Hancock's Half-Hour* and *Fawlty Towers*, and in America *The Dick Van Dyke Show*, *The Phil Silvers Show* (*Sgt Bilko*), *Taxi*, *Cheers*, *M*A*S*H* and *Modern Family*.

Hay Fever, *Private Lives*, *A Midsummer Night's Dream*, *Pygmalion*, *The Government Inspector*, *She Stoops to Conquer* ... these plays are situation comedies. So are the best farces, as John Mortimer pointed out to me when we worked together on the script of *A Little Hotel*.

John had written the first draft, and I invited him over to lunch in Hampstead Garden Suburb to discuss rewrites. When he was already on his way Peter Hall phoned: the NT was re-scheduling the play and rehearsals were to be postponed for three months. John was an exceedingly busy man, a QC, a board member of the NT and the Royal Court, a prolific author and so forth, so on his arrival I told him that our work was no longer urgent. 'But do come in if you like.'

'Hmm, smells delicious,' he said, sniffing and ambling past me into the kitchen like a slightly lame and myopic bloodhound. 'Hello,' he said to my wife, Rita.

'Hello John,' she said with a welcoming smile. 'Would you like some roast lamb, roast potatoes and runner beans?'

'Hmm, I think I would,' he said, and behind his thick spectacles I saw that his eyes had fixed on an opened bottle of good claret on the kitchen counter. They gleamed. 'Is this for lunch too?'

'Yes,' I said.

'I'll stay,' he said. We ate and drank, and went through my notes. I was excited. I could hardly believe that I was working with a writer whom I so admired, the creator of *Rumpole of the Bailey*. *Yes Minister* had changed my life.

I asked him about *A Flea in Her Ear*, the first Feydeau farce he had translated for the NT, for Olivier and Tynan, directed by Jacques Charon of the Comédie Française. He explained that the first act wasn't very funny in the original French, consisting mainly of exposition that sets everything up for the big laughs in Act Two and Act Three. But, because modern audiences are not particularly patient, he had laboured mightily to put in a lot of new funny lines, jokes, epigrams, anything he could think of to make the text sparkle. 'And which line got the biggest laugh?' I asked.

'Ah. That was in Act Three, actually, when Alby Finney said "*What?*" At that moment, everything that he had not understood was suddenly revealed to him.' A situational laugh, in fact.

101. If you value your privacy, try to make your work famous and yourself unknown.

Privacy is an excellent by-product of the patronising attitude towards TV comedy writing. Trish Eddington, Paul's wife, used to go to our butcher, Mr Daniels, at the bottom of Muswell Hill. Sometimes she'd see my wife there. Mr Daniels, a kind and friendly man, always congratulated Trish on Paul's success in the show. Then he turned to Rita.

'How's yer old man, Rita? Haven't seen him on the telly much recently. Does he get any work now?'

'He's doing really well,' Rita said. 'He writes the show that Paul is in.'

'You're a brave girl,' said Mr Daniels. 'I've put in an extra chop for you.'

The Public Lending Right started up around then. The idea was that authors should earn royalties on books borrowed from public libraries; before this, hundreds of people might read the same copy of the book, while the author got paid for just one sale. Everyone saw that this was unfair, except for the Library Association: librarians opposed the PLR, because it meant more work for them. Also, it was obvious to them that it is librarians, not authors, who are essential to libraries.

We applied for royalties for the *Yes Minister* books, subtitled *The Diaries of a Cabinet Minister, by the Rt Hon. Jim Hacker MP, edited by Lynn and Jay*, and received a letter pointing out that Mr Hacker was the author. As editors, it said, we were not entitled to royalty payments unless we could demonstrate that we had made a significant contribution to the writing of the books. I wrote back and asked if I could publish their letter. I received no reply.

Shortly afterwards, the first cheque arrived.

The second and third series of *Yes Minister* were each more successful than the last. Each time Nigel and Sydney Lotterby or Peter Whitmore won BAFTA Awards for our show, and each time we were not invited. We won the Broadcasting Press Guild Award twice, and we didn't even know about it until Paul, who was always gracious, rang my front-door bell, handed me the certificate and said, 'I think this really belongs to you and Tony.'

At the end of the third series, having written twenty-one episodes, we felt ready to stop. We asked for a lot more money and we didn't hide our view that writers were disrespected by the BBC hierarchy, who had it in their power to change the perception of the writer's pre-eminent contribution to television programmes. The BBC wanted us to continue, but it was not willing to step up financially. We didn't mind stopping. Tony's company Video Arts was going from strength to strength, and I had been directing at the National Theatre and in the West End. We set what we thought was a fair price and waited. We asked for ten thousand pounds per script – that is, five thousand pounds each, a pittance by today's standards, but it was more than the BBC had ever paid to a pair of situation-comedy writers and they didn't see why they should.

We, on the other hand, didn't see why we should go on writing. We had said everything we wanted to say. We were satisfied.

* * *

I first went to Los Angeles in 1983, just after Tony and I finished writing the third and last series of *Yes Minister*. I had been brought there from London, especially to meet John Landis.

A couple of weeks earlier Peter Guber, the famous movie mogul, was in London, and my agent sent me to meet him. He talked very fast, he had superhuman energy, a very short attention span and he had been President of Columbia Pictures at the age of only twenty-seven. Within a few minutes of our ordering coffee, during which time I had barely spoken, he told me that he had the perfect project for me. I wondered how he could know that. John Landis the famous director, he told me, was developing a film called *Clue*, based on the famous board game, and needed someone to write the script. I didn't feel famous enough.[29]

I knew the game. I had enjoyed it when I was seven or

---

29 It turned out I was right about that. I eventually was told that no fewer than five previous writers, including Tom Stoppard, had been hired for this job and had subsequently had the sense to withdraw from it.

eight. In England it was called Cluedo. It took place in a house rather like the one in which I grew up, with a big square hall, a magnificent staircase, a conservatory and a basement which I had always hoped contained secret passages. But I was sceptical. A board game has no story, just a setting and some characters; not even characters, really, because they were without characterisation; they were merely *names* of characters.

I was not in the film business. I had written one film that had been made, a decade earlier, *The Internecine Project*,[30] starring James Coburn, Lee Grant and Keenan Wynn. The director made a number of changes without consulting me, and I hadn't liked the result. I had seen only one of John Landis's films, *Animal House*. It was like no other film that I'd ever seen, two hours of sustained hilarious madness. I loved it.

In spite of my doubts about a film based on a board game, I wanted to meet him. I had a free week, I had never been to the West Coast and I wanted to see LA. Most of all, I wanted to fly first class once in my life, and it appeared that Universal would pay. Later I discovered it was a provision of the Writers' Guild basic agreement, but I took it as generosity by the studio (I would learn about studios eventually). Everything about the trip itself excited my curiosity, except writing the film.

I was booked in at the Chateau Marmont Hotel. It was fairly run-down in those days. I didn't know that Landis's friend John Belushi, the brilliant star of *Animal House*, had recently died in the hotel. I'd heard about all the freeways but

---

30 Not my title, I hasten to add.

I hadn't realised that without a car I'd be a virtual prisoner in my room. I hadn't brought my driving licence.

There was no restaurant and no room service except sand-wiches, but after the longest flight I'd ever taken I was happy just to sleep. The next morning a teamster drove me to Todd AO, a post-production sound stage somewhere in Holly-wood. John was mixing his seminal music video, *Thriller*. Not having worked in films I had never seen such a place: a huge cinema with a pool table and a ping-pong table where the front seats usually were, and, in the centre of the enorm-ous room, a mixing desk on a raised level which Landis be-strode, shouting commands, telling stories, cracking jokes and simultaneously running the sound mix.

He was about six foot, slim, bearded and bespectacled, and yet his manner and his walk were slightly reminiscent of Groucho Marx. Curiously, he wore a jacket and a tie, and to this day I don't think I've seen him in anything else. Apart from a few grey hairs and a little extra weight, he looks exactly the same today. He was welcoming, exuded massive energy and bonhomie, and introduced me to abso-lutely everyone in the room. I didn't catch their names. A little later, a nice-looking African-American kid offered to get pizza for everyone. It was a while before I realised that the nice-looking kid was Michael Jackson.

Instead, we went across the street for lunch, to a greasy spoon that is now a trendy restaurant. I discovered that John was as knowledgeable about London as I was ignorant about LA. We knew actors in common, like Lila Kaye (with whom I'd worked at the RSC), who had been in his film *An Amer-ican Werewolf in London*. He had strong views about British theatre, British films, Mrs Thatcher, Evelyn Waugh (whom he said had written the best novel ever written about LA, *The*

Loved One) – in fact, he had strong views about everything. He was opinionated, entertaining, confident and extremely well read. I was intimidated.

He didn't want to talk about *Clue*; he was too involved in his mix that day. We arranged that I'd meet him the next day in his office, and he would tell me what he wanted. There was nothing for me to do except wait and see, and I was driven back to the Chateau. I wandered along Sunset, past the giant smoking Marlboro Man billboard (I could see the back of it from my hotel room), past a distinctly un-British British pub called Oscars, past some strip malls and a railroad carriage called Carneys that sold hot dogs, and I wondered if the neighbourhood was safe. There was no way to tell that Sunset Strip was in one of the fanciest places in the city. I asked where the city centre was, but nobody seemed able to tell me.

That evening I was taken to dinner by Lori, a young woman, who was called Vice-President of the Guber-Peters Entertainment Company. I assumed, with that title, she was pretty important. We went to the Japanese restaurant next door to the Chateau, and I ate sushi for the first time. I pretended I liked raw fish.

The next day my teamster took me to John Landis's office at Universal. Debra Hill, the actual producer of the film, was there too. John welcomed me with enormous enthusiasm, as is his custom, sat me down in his office and pitched his idea to me.

I had never heard a pitch before. In England we didn't 'pitch'. It's a cliché that the Brits understate everything and the Americans overstate everything, but it's true nonetheless. In London one might suggest one had an amusing little idea that might be worth consideration; I soon learned that if you did such a thing in Hollywood they would show you the door. The minimum word of praise for an idea, even one's own idea, *especially* one's own idea, is 'great'.

102. Learn to pitch.

John's pitch was like nothing I have ever seen, before or since. He acted out his vision of the movie: up on his feet shouting, running, gasping, whispering, screaming when a body was discovered, careering around the office to demonstrate how the characters would rush around the house, jumping up on his desk, a whirlwind of high-octane activity. I was mesmerised, fascinated and drawn right into the bizarre, mysterious tale that he was weaving. Finally, after about fifteen minutes, he stopped and said: 'And then the Butler says: "I know who did it." And he tells us!'

He paused dramatically. I waited, eager to know the explanation. It would have to be remarkably ingenious. But he said nothing.

'So, who did?' I asked.

'I don't know!' he said. 'That's why I need a writer!'

103. Character is plot.

My head was spinning as I was driven back to the Chateau Marmont. The problem was, although there was a story, there was actually *no* story. Graham Greene once observed that character is plot, and here there was no plot because there were no defined characters. Just colours: Colonel Mustard, Miss Scarlet, Professor Plum and so forth.

It was a series of events – admittedly potentially funny events – but without an explanation or a connecting thread. There was no reason for any of it to happen. The names made no realistic sense, there was no character development, just some weapons and a floor plan of the ground floor of a mansion. There was nothing to work from. I couldn't see where to begin. What would the story be *about*?

John and his wife Deborah, a notable costume designer, took me out to a Japanese restaurant that night. They picked me up at the Chateau – I had asked Landis if he knew where it was, and he had given me a quizzical look as if I was slightly deranged. Clearly everyone knew where it was, except the stoned limo driver who'd collected me at the airport. John told me that John Belushi had died there, and through the brash, wisecracking exterior I saw real anguish as he talked about a friend he had loved.

We ate sushi. Again I pretended I liked it. I didn't say much. I was shy, jet-lagged and in a writing fog. All night I stayed awake and tried to think out a way through the maze; and after some hours a few tenuous thoughts occurred. So I phoned John's office in the morning and he asked me to come over at lunchtime. When I arrived he had thoughtfully ordered in some sushi and hospitably insisted that I ate some more raw fish. I was beginning to feel like a dolphin.

I started to outline my sketchy thoughts, and as soon as I said something that he liked he leaped to his feet to start riffing on it. My ideas were too feeble to withstand the Landis treatment, so I said, 'You talked at yesterday's meeting, now it's my turn.' Guiltily, clapping his hand over his mouth like a small boy, he sat right down again. But his eyes were still gleaming enthusiastically through his specs.

I talked for a few minutes, trying to develop my thoughts, then lurched to a halt. 'I'm afraid that's all I've got so far,' I said.

'Can I talk now?' he asked.

'Of course,' I said. He asked me some good questions and together we came up with a few more thoughts. 'Okay,' he said, suddenly. 'I'd like you to write it.' I was both pleased and horrified. I had two or three pages of loosely spaced notes plus a written copy of his pitch. Not much to base a script on. Not much at all.

We shook hands warmly and said we'd be in touch.

That night Debra Hill, the producer, took me out for sushi. I demanded a steak. Next day I was on the plane home.

The afternoon before I left on the 'redeye' to London, John set up a screening so that I could see his latest film, *Trading Places*. It was superb. High comedy, a film about the class system in America, satirical in tone about the 'nature versus nurture' debate, wonderfully acted by everyone, beautiful to look at. There was, however, a long sequence on the subway involving a real gorilla and Dan Aykroyd in a gorilla suit. It had nothing to do with the main story and could easily have been cut. I couldn't see why it was there, since I'd always been told that an essential skill of screenwriting is to stay on story, always.

104. Don't throw out a sequence with big laughs simply to stay on story.

Everyone who teaches screenwriting emphasises that, above all else, you must stay 'on story'. Every executive I have ever met believes this. It is not true. Comedy is the exception to this rule.

Five or six huge movie-theatre-rocking laughs means you probably will have a hit. Ten of them means that you certainly will. When I first saw *Trading Places*, alone in a screening room, I thought that sequence should be cut. When I saw it with an audience a month later I changed my mind.

This is why film critics ought to see films with an audience, as theatre critics do. But mostly, they won't. They don't want the group experience, which always was and still is how comedy plays best.

I wanted to write a film for Landis. I felt I had a lot to learn from him. The music under the titles was the Overture to *La Nozze di Figaro*. I was surprised that John knew it, as he had told me that he had dropped out of high school. I shouldn't have been, because I'd seen his extensive library, and discovered that not only had he read every book in it, he remembered them all and could quote from them.

Four or five weeks later my production of Joe Orton's *Loot* opened at the Lyric Theatre on Shaftesbury Avenue. That night a bottle of Dom Perignon arrived at the stage door from John and Deborah. What struck me even more than their characteristic generosity was that John had remembered something that I'd mentioned only once, taking place so far away.

* * *

Back at home, faced with writing the actual script, I was at a loss for quite a while. I needed a starting point for my story. A house party, murder-mystery comedy had to be a parody of an Agatha Christie whodunnit.

105. Pastiche/parody. Keep them short. Ninety minutes, tops.[31]

Clue is a short film. It has to be, because it is a parody.

It also had to be a period film. I set it in the only period

---

31 The same applies to animated films. All of the great feature films that Walt Disney himself made last about eighty minutes. Now they make two-hour animated films! Children can't sit still and pay attention for as long as that.

of modern American history that I really knew about: the McCarthy era. I thought back to 1965, when I had met the great Donald Ogden Stewart.

1965 was a comparatively innocent time, before hijacking, before diplomats were targets, before suicide bombers. Embassies were not the fortresses that they are today. The library at the American embassy in London was a showpiece and open to academics and research people. Lots of people used it. As the Vietnam War went from bad to worse, the State Department made economies and announced that the library was to be closed. This caused an outcry in the British press: not only were the Americans bombing and napalming North Vietnam, they were shutting down libraries! In response, the cultural attaché decided to use the remainder of his annual library budget to put on a Festival of American Arts in the embassy's auditorium.

The main purpose of the Festival was to get famous American visitors to perform there while visiting London. Isaac Stern gave a recital, Barbra Streisand (who had not yet opened in *Funny Girl* in London) gave a concert, Cy Coleman sat at the piano and played the score for a new, unproduced musical he'd written called *Sweet Charity*. George Mully, the American expatriate director of the festival and a friend of mine, wanted some original programming and decided to devise two evenings of American literary humour. The first was to start with Ben Franklin and get as far as Ambrose Bierce by way of Mark Twain. The second evening was to start with H. L. Mencken and cover great twentieth-century humorists including, of course, James Thurber, Dorothy Parker, Robert Benchley, Ring Lardner, Leo Q. Ross and others too numerous to mention here.

Then George discovered, through his friend Larry Adler,

the world-famous mouth-organ player who was an American refugee from McCarthyism, that Donald Ogden Stewart was living in Hampstead.

In his day, Don Stewart was a legend. Like Thurber, he hailed from Columbus, Ohio. He went to Yale on a scholarship. By the time he was in his late twenties he had run with the bulls in Pamplona with Hemingway and appeared as a character in *The Sun Also Rises*, written four best-selling books, a hit Broadway play, *Rebound*, and the musical *Fine and Dandy*. One of the original members of the famous Algonquin round table, he was on the staff of *The New Yorker*. 'Did you know Dorothy Parker?' I asked him.

'Toots, we shared an office,' he said. He called everybody he liked 'Toots', men and women alike.

'So you knew her quite well?'

'Let me put it this way. If the office had been any smaller we'd have had to get married.'

Soon Don went out to Hollywood. He hung out by the pool with Robert Benchley – 'Let's get out of these wet things and into a dry Martini.' He wrote dozens of movies, and won the Oscar in 1940 for his glorious screenplay for *The Philadelphia Story*. He met a tough Australian woman, Ella Winter, the widow of the great, muckraking journalist Lincoln Steffens, who had been to the Soviet Union and famously remarked, 'I have seen the future and it works.' This fatuous statement was considered wise and important in the thirties by all those intellectual fellow-travellers, like George Bernard Shaw, whom Stalin called useful idiots.

In spite of his political naivety, however, Steffens did much good, and was instrumental in drawing attention to the poverty and injustice suffered by the itinerant grape-pickers in California, who became the subject of John Steinbeck's masterpiece *The Grapes of Wrath*. Ella called herself a communist, and so did Don.

106. Know your subject and the background against which the script takes place.

Don was a founding member of the Screenwriters' Guild in 1933 and President of the Anti-Nazi League, and so when the Red Scare hit America after the Cold War began and Senator Joe McCarthy went on the rampage, Don was blacklisted. This could only be revoked if he agreed to name names in front of the House Un-American Activities Committee. It was 1952. He was on tour in New Haven with a new play for Broadway called *The Kidders*. He packed his bags and left for London. His play closed on the road. He never returned. His career was over. Apart from a fascinating but ultimately sad autobiography, *By a Stroke of Luck!*, he never wrote another word. Far from being un-American, he was so profoundly American that, away from home, he simply couldn't write.

Don was elegant, willowy, graceful and welcoming. He was initially hesitant about getting involved with a performance at the US Embassy because, although he never let it show, he was bitter about the way he had been treated as a traitor by his country. But George persuaded him to turn up and be the MC of both compilations.

For fourteen years Don had been hanging out in his beautiful Georgian mansion in Hampstead, drinking too much and hosting American expatriates from all over Europe. At various afternoon teas there my girlfriend Rita and I met some distinguished 'subversives': Charlie and Oona Chaplin, Ring Lardner Jr, Waldo Salt, Joseph Losey, Carl Foreman and

many other blacklisted and exiled Americans. You have never met a bunch of angrier, more erudite, literate, civilised
and confused men and women. I had already learned a lot
about this shameful period in recent American history, but
this was an ongoing education. Non-blacklisted American
friends with guts also showed up regularly at their house,
notably Katharine Hepburn who came to stay every year. Although I could never understand how any of them could
have been apologists for Stalin, which almost all of them
had been (apart from Hepburn), it was clear that this had
been caused by a combination of ignorance, denial and mis-
placed idealism. The notion that any of them were a threat
to the United States was simply ridiculous. Hepburn said in
her foreword to Don's autobiography: 'He laughed his way
to the top of the heap and looked down. Saw the bottom of
the heap and thought "this is not fair". He forsook his giddy
companions for serious thinking and had to leave the country of his birth.' Serious but flawed thinking, she might have
said, though perhaps not in a foreword to his book.

While I was in New York with *Cambridge Circus*, Jack Gilford, a great American comedy actor whom I'd seen in *A
Funny Thing Happened on the Way to the Forum* with his close
friend Zero Mostel, came to see it with his wife Madeleine.
A few days later they invited me for dinner. I was thrilled.
They'd been married about fifty years and he always referred
to her as 'The First Mrs Gilford'. He told me the story of how,
when *Forum* was in trouble on the road before opening in
New York, the producer Harold Prince had suggested bring-
ing Jerome Robbins in to help the ageing director, George
Abbott. Robbins's intervention led to the creation of the
show-stopping opening number 'Comedy Tonight'. What
many people didn't realise was that Robbins had named

names to the House Un-American Activities Committee, whereas Mostel had refused to name anybody and had been blacklisted for many years as a result. When asked during the House hearing, which was televised, if he had anything to say after pleading the Fifth Amendment, Mostel had replied: 'I would like to thank this committee for giving me my first chance to appear on television in five years.'[32]

Larry Gelbart, whom I later got to know fairly well, told me about the troubles *Forum* had on the road. 'All I can say is, if Hitler is still alive I hope he's on the road with a musical.'[33]

Harold Prince, Jack Gilford told me, had gone to Mostel to ask if he would work with Robbins. Jack was really proud of his friend Zero's reply: 'Yes. I will not have dinner with him but I will work with him. We on the left have no blacklist.' According to Robbins's biographer,[34] Mostel said nothing about the past when they met in the rehearsal room, apart from his opening line: 'Hello, Loose-Lips.'[35] These enmities never went away.

Seventeen years later, in 1983, I started writing *Clue* with Graham Greene's 'character is plot' rule in mind. He meant, I think, that plot *follows from* character. Characters dictate the plot. If the plot is not driven by the inevitability of who the characters are and what they want, you will get a mechanically driven script. So who were these people by the name of Mr Green, Professor Plum, Miss Scarlet, Mrs Peacock, Mrs White and Colonel Mustard? Those couldn't be their real

---

32 Angry joke.
33 Another angry joke.
34 *Jerome Robbins – His Life, His Theater, His Dance*, by Deborah Jowitt.
35 More barely repressed anger.

names, they had to be aliases. And, to avoid coincidence, the aliases had to have been assigned to them by the same person.

Why did they need aliases? Perhaps because they were all being blackmailed. By whom? It followed that the person who gave them the aliases had to be the murderer. The winner of the board game is the player who is first to find out who killed Mr Boddy, in which room and with which weapon.[36] It seemed that a logical answer would be that Mr Boddy would not only be the murder victim, but also the blackmailer who invited them to the house.

What were they all being blackmailed about? Into this familiar framework I placed McCarthyism. This meant that the year was about 1954. This meant using fifties-style music. It suggested that what the characters, all of whom had some dark secret to hide, could have in common was some connection with Washington DC. Although *Clue* had to be as light as a soufflé, like all farce (or broad comedy, as they call farce in the movie world), it needed a weighty basis for the plot. Having worked on my West End production of Joe Orton's *Loot*, I felt inspired to make *Clue* as epigrammatic and as dark as I could, bearing in mind it had to be a 'family' film. The hideous dilemma was obvious, and the same for all the characters: who is the murderer and how do I find out who it is before he or she kills me?

I had to keep two important rules in mind:

107. Don't call it satire.

Satire, according to the dictionary, is a mode of literature that

---

36   In the English version of the game, Cluedo, Mr Boddy is Dr Black and Mr Green is the Revd Green.

uses comedy, wit or humour with the intention of changing society. *Clue* was full of political and satirical jokes about McCarthyism and the Red Scare, but it was not a satire, even though some of the jokes were satirical. That was not because it was a period film: *M*A*S*H* was made in the late sixties and, although it was a period film set during the Korean War, it was surely intended to be satirical about contemporaneous events in Vietnam. *Clue* was clearly not written with the intention of changing society.

Tony Jay doesn't describe *Yes Minister* and *Yes Prime Minister* as satire. He believes that because we offer observations on (rather than solutions to) society's ills and injustices, we are not trying to change anything. My opinion is different: I don't believe that satirical writing has to offer solutions – at least, not practical ones. If that were so, Jonathan Swift's pamphlet *A Modest Proposal* would not be satirical. It proposed a solution to the problem of the Irish famine: that they eat all the babies. I think that *Yes Minister* is satirical, but not in the modern British *TW3* and *Spitting Image* sense of impersonating and lampooning identifiable real people. I was happy, however, not to describe it as such. If your work is described as satire, it may get you accolades that other comedy writers don't get. But it can substantially reduce your viewing figures and box office.

George S. Kaufman, the great Broadway playwright and director, and screenwriter, once said: 'Satire is what closes on Saturday night.' An excellent wisecrack, but it led the way to a general belief in America that satire is not commercial. When you pitch a satirical film idea, don't refer to it as satire. I used to, and I was met with the inevitable response that satirical films don't make money. This view is factually incorrect. Plenty have done so, if budgeted right. They may not be blockbusters, but there always was and still is an audience for them, and sometimes a very big audience: *Thank You for Smoking, Wag the Dog, Election, Broadcast News*, my film *The Distinguished Gentleman, Being There, Network, The Graduate, Dr Strangelove, The Apartment* . . . Their producers were wise enough not to advertise them as satires.

The second rule that I realised in writing *Clue* is:

108. The arc of the character doesn't matter in parody.

Graham Greene's dictum that character is plot means that characters, and how they develop in relation to each other and the story (known in Hollywood as 'the arc of the character'), are what holds the audience's interest over a longer evening. Parody and pastiche don't give you that advantage. They contain no depth. They are, in effect, elongated sketches. Therefore you must be outstandingly inventive with your jokes, as in *Airplane!, Blazing Saddles* and *Young Frankenstein*, in order to hold your audience. And remembering Rule 105, you would be wise to see that it lasts no more than ninety minutes. Preferably somewhat less! (I don't include those incredibly long end credits in the timing, as no one ever waits to read them unless they are in the film industry.)

109. Get the story structure in shape before starting to write the script.

You must at least know the beginning, the middle and how it ends. Approximately, at least.

Some months later I delivered the script. It had taken a long time to think out the plot and give some dimension to the characters, to find – in effect – the explanation for what

John had pitched so dramatically. As always for me, the story and structure were the difficult part. After taking months to think it out I wrote the screenplay very quickly, in three bursts of one week each, between writing *Yes Prime Minister* with Tony and directing *Loot* in the West End and John Mortimer's translation of Georges Feydeau's *A Little Hotel on the Side* at the NT. These plays gave me, among other things, further insights into the logic required of farce.

The script contained many satirical jokes. America was and still is totally hostile to anything that can remotely be described as 'socialist'. Most Americans are still phobic about socialism, though they have little idea of what the word means. Wadsworth the Butler, who (I decided) was Mr Boddy's butler, reveals that Mr Boddy regarded them all as un-American. Wadsworth confesses tearfully that his dark secret, for which he was paying blackmail, was that 'my wife had friends who were . . . socialists!' Everyone present gasps in horror.

Mr Green has to confess he's gay. Even with the repeal of 'Don't Ask, Don't Tell', it is still remarkable that in the US, at the time of writing this book, there are no openly gay senators, governors, members of the Cabinet or Justices of the Supreme Court, and only four openly gay members of the House of Representatives. Even today, it would probably ruin Mr Green's career in the State Department if he came out. Colonel Mustard was revealed to be a war profiteer, but he was very small-time if compared to Halliburton and Vice-President Cheney. Mrs Peacock's husband was a corrupt senator whose husband sold his votes to rich lobbyists – this would describe virtually every member of the Senate today.

In fact, Wadsworth defends Mr Boddy's blackmail. 'He decided to turn his information to good use and make a little money out of it. What could be more American than that? Mr Boddy was truly an apostle of free enterprise.' Political jokes were all over the script:

Wadsworth Professor Plum, you were once a Professor of Psychiatry specializing in helping paranoid and homicidal lunatics suffering from delusions of grandeur.
Professor Plum Yes, but now I work at the United Nations.
Wadsworth So your work has not changed.

110. American studios think that 'broad' comedies are stupid comedies.

A mixture of intelligence and broad comedy had not been common in recent American films, except John's. They are today regarded as mutually exclusive by the studios, who are dumbing everything down. Looking back, I realise that the script contained another stylistic mixture typical of a Landis film: comedy and horror. I had done my best with a difficult task, but I expected it to be rejected out of hand as either too intelligent or too silly. I could have argued both cases.

To my relief and astonishment, John, Debra Hill and Peter Guber all liked it a lot. By then, however, John was becoming distracted by other film ideas. He wasn't sure that he wanted to direct it but, showing once again an amazing generosity of spirit, he asked me if I would like to. If so, he would be an executive producer and do all that he could to make it happen. He did, and it did. I shall always be grateful to him. It was not the film that I would have chosen as my first, but it was the one that came along.

* * *

After two and a half years of pointless negotiations, the BBC met our price and we agreed to continue the series with Jim as Prime Minister. This enabled us to write about foreign affairs, defence, nuclear weapons, MI5, the appointment of bishops and other subjects that would have been outside his purview as Minister of Administrative Affairs. But more negotiations followed, this time with the actors: Paul and Nigel declared that they would not do *Yes Prime Minister* unless we dispensed with the studio audience. Very well, we said, no more shows. After a while a summit conference was held with the actors. Tony and I were inflexible because we were always aware of the possibility of political interference.

111. Political comedy on television should be performed in front of a studio audience.

Without an audience it would be all too easy for a high-ranking politician or civil servant to call the Chairman or the Director-General, complain that the show was not funny and exert pressure to have it taken off the air. Three hundred people, randomly chosen, watching in the studio and laughing their heads off was our insurance policy. The government could not claim that it was not funny. Eventually Paul and Nigel saw our point.

Our opinion at the time was that the studio audience allows the solitary viewer at home the same permission to laugh out loud without embarrassment. I'm no longer sure that this is true, and the studio audience certainly seems off-putting to some people. However, this is mainly because journalists who think they know keep referring to the sound of the audience as a 'laugh track', implying that the laughter is faked. This may be true of some American TV shows, but it was emphatically not the case at the BBC. If a line didn't get a laugh, it didn't get a laugh!

Then, at the last minute, *Yes Prime Minister* nearly didn't happen because the BBC was too cheap to provide Paul with a car to get him to and from rehearsals. His health was visibly starting to fail; he had all kinds of problems caused by what turned out to be skin cancer. They wouldn't provide it for him, and finally he gave in. I thought they were most ungenerous, but they said they couldn't do it because it would create a precedent. As Jim Hacker said in the show: 'You mean, you can't do the right thing now because it might mean that you have to do the right thing next time?' Paul said that line with relish.

To their credit, the BBC had behaved impeccably when we wrote an episode, 'The Challenge', showing how it can be pressured by the government into dropping a programme or a news item that Whitehall or Number 10 doesn't like. There is a myth, cultivated by both the government and the BBC, that the BBC is independent; but since it gets all its money from the licence fee, controlled by government legislation and renewed every few years, it isn't. When we sent in the script we got a call from Syd Lotterby. 'Um . . . I've read the last scene and I have to show it to the Head of Comedy.'

'Of course,' we said. 'Go right ahead.'

It wasn't long before we heard from John Howard Davies. 'I've read "The Challenge"', he said cheerfully. 'Very funny. But I can't not mention it to the Powers That Be. So I'm going to phone them the day it goes on the air and warn them, just in case there are questions in Parliament or from the press.'

This was an intelligent move. He knew that he couldn't suppress the show, even if he had wanted to (which I'm sure he didn't). If he had tried, we would have leaked that the BBC, which allowed us to criticise and make fun of everything else in public life, couldn't take a joke against itself. Nothing further was said. The show was recorded as written. John phoned Bill Cotton, Managing Director of BBC TV, Aubrey Singer (Director of Special Projects) and Alasdair Milne (the Director-General). They all watched it for the first time when it was transmitted.

The next day we got three phone calls. I heard first from Bill. He was very jovial. 'Saw the show last night. Loved it. Tell me, was that BBC chap meant to be Aubrey or Alasdair?' Tony heard from Aubrey Singer; he loved it too, but wanted to know if the BBC official was meant to be Alasdair or Bill. You can guess the question that was in Alasdair's message.

The upshot was that the BBC emerged with total credit, in our eyes and everyone else's. There were no questions asked, because what we were saying was obviously true, but they had behaved like grown-ups and they hadn't tried to censor us. I can think of no other television company in the world that would behave with such good grace and common sense. I hope that it would be the same today, but I'm not sure.

112. Truth is not only funnier than fiction (see Rule 99), it is frequently stranger than fiction.

Tony and I had lots of ideas for *Yes Prime Minister*. One of my favourites turned into an episode called 'One of Us', in which Sir Humphrey was suspected of being a Russian double agent. It was based on the notion that Sir Roger Hollis, the former Head of MI5, might have been the fifth man in the Burgess, Maclean, Philby and Anthony Blunt spy ring.

Rita and I were friends with General Dick Lloyd, who had been Director of Military Intelligence for many years. He was slight and wiry, with a scar on his cheek from Arnhem and piercing blue eyes beneath bushy eyebrows. I referred to him as M. After dinner one weekend when we stayed with the Lloyds in Lymington, I asked Dick if he knew Roger Hollis.

'I knew him as well as anybody,' he said.

'Oh, pretty well?'

'Hardly at all.'

'So – was he a spy for them or for us?'

'Doesn't make much difference. All spies are on both sides.'

'What do you mean?'

'When you discover that you have a foreign agent in your midst, the last thing you want to do is expose him, arrest him, put him on trial, make a big show of it, then put him in prison. That's what the press and the politicians want you to do, but you only do it if you have no real alternative. Arresting and imprisoning a spy is an admission of defeat.

'What you want to do is to turn him. Make him a double agent. Well, obviously you can't turn a spy unless you give him some information to send back to his controller. And you can't give him false or useless information to send home, because the other side aren't idiots, they already know a lot about you, and they'd quickly realise their agent had been turned. So, what do you do? You give him *real* information, *real* secrets – but you try to give them stuff that, finally, is not vital to your national interests.

'The problem is, that's mostly a matter of opinion. So, you see, everyone of any importance in intelligence and counter-intelligence is a double agent. The real question is, *ultimately* whose side are they on?'

I asked whose side Sir Roger Hollis was ultimately on. The General said, 'In my opinion, Hollis was one of their chaps. But we'll probably never know.'

'That's a calamity! The head of MI5!'

General Lloyd seemed unperturbed. 'Well, there is another way of looking at it,' he remarked. 'Virtually all wars start by accident. Look at the First World War. Nobody wanted that. Hitler wouldn't have invaded Poland if he knew that we'd declare war – why would he think we'd do that, we'd tolerated the annexation of Czechoslovakia. Even the Falklands War began because Argentina misunderstood warning signals from the FO. So you could argue that the more we all know about each other, the better. If we know their secrets and they know ours, the world will be a safer place.'

113. You are not responsible for who likes your show.

You can't select your fans. When your programme is on TV, people whom you might not like might like you.

The series was becoming ever more popular. Margaret Thatcher let it be known that it was her favourite programme. Tony was happy about this but it bothered me; I told everyone I met that we'd had enthusiastic responses from Tony Benn, Roy Hattersley and Gerald Kaufman as well. I didn't necessarily admire them more, but they were from the other party and it seemed to me that the PM was trying to co-opt the popularity of the show in support of Thatcherism.

We were invited to parties and dinner at Number 10, where we met people who had been carefully chosen to connect with one another because of similar interests. Like Terry Wogan and Isaiah Berlin, for instance. At one large cocktail party Mrs Thatcher stood in the Yellow State Room and formally welcomed us. It was not one of her better speeches: 'In this very room', she said, 'the Duke of Wellington walked up and down as he worried about the Battle of Waterloo; in this very room Winston . . .' (surely she couldn't have known him) '. . . Winston walked up and down as he worried about the outcome of the Battle of Britain; and in this very room *I* walked up and down as I worried and fretted about our troops in the Falklands War. And all of you, by being here tonight in this room, are footnotes in the pages of history.'

I was standing next to Michael Winner, the loud film producer. 'Well!' he said, making no attempt to lower his voice. 'I thought everyone 'ere was doin' well, but it turns out we're just a bunch of fuckin' footnotes!'

Denis Thatcher had clearly had enough. The invitations said 'Carriages at 8pm'. At ten to eight Denis walked around the room, gazing at his wristwatch, saying loudly to nobody in particular, 'My God! It's ten to eight! It's ten to eight! God, look at the time!'

114. Approve all translations. Why not?

The books were being translated into a number of languages. We had the right to approve the translations, and every now and again galleys in Spanish, Portuguese, Hebrew, Russian and even Chinese would thud through the mailbox. I had no idea how our work had been translated, and there was no way to find out short of becoming fluent in a great many languages very fast. Naturally, I approved them. Tony did the same. I often wondered what was in them, though.

The TV shows were now being shown in fifty-four countries.[37] In the Middle East it was popular in Israel, Jordan and Saudi Arabia; it was big in the Soviet Union, where presumably it was seen by the authorities as an attack on Western democracies, while the general population probably saw it as an attack on bureaucracy. In China, where it was dubbed, TV viewers had the opportunity to see our mandarins speaking Mandarin.

115. Many people think that the actors make it up as they go along.

It's like believing what you read in the newspapers: you know you shouldn't, but you do. That was obviously what Mr Daniels, our butcher, thought. No doubt that's why Mrs Thatcher rewarded Paul and Nigel with a matched set of CBEs in the New Year's Honours List that year, and not us.

Then, the following New Year's Day, I awoke to the news that Tony was to be knighted; it was for doing favours for the Thatcher government, including writing speeches for Geoffrey Howe and Nigel Lawson, and creating a party political broadcast for Mrs Thatcher that turned the general election around and contributed to her third victory. Tony's work behind the scenes for Thatcherism was barely known at that time and I had always urged Tony, for the sake of *Yes Minister*, to keep it discreet. I'm sure that he would have anyway. Now the cat was out of the bag, but it didn't seem to matter.

---

37 By 2011, eighty-four countries.

116. Award ceremonies are simply a sales tool.

One day, when *Yes Prime Minister* was an even bigger hit than *Yes Minister*, I finally got a phone call from Bill Cotton's office inviting me to the BAFTA Awards. It was several years too late and I declined. A couple of weeks later his secretary phoned again, saying that perhaps I hadn't understood that Bill was inviting me to be his guest at his table. I thanked her and explained that I'd lost interest. A week later Bill phoned me himself. 'Are you coming to the BAFTA Awards? It's really important that you're there.'

'Why?'

'Because – look, I want you to be there. And Tony.'

'Have you asked him?'

'Yes, he says he's not coming. Can you get him to come?'

'I doubt it.'

'You must.'

I paused, and considered. 'Are you trying to tell me we've won something?'

'You know I can't say that, it's all secret 'til the night.'

'Bill,' I said, 'let me explain something to you. Tony hates awards ceremonies. If I twist his arm and make him come, and he doesn't win anything . . . you'll have hell to pay.'

'No problem,' said Bill. 'Just get him there.' We were about to hang up when Bill added: 'Oh, one more thing. Look surprised, okay?'

On the evening of the awards, we were there. It was announced that we had won one of the special awards, the BAFTA Writer's Award. We both looked suitably astonished. We had carefully prepared a joke that would look ad-libbed and incredibly witty, but at the moment we reached the mic and I opened my mouth to speak, the orchestra struck up a fanfare. It must have looked pretty funny. There were profuse apologies for this afterwards, but it was an apt metaphor.

117. Try to resist if the Prime Minister wants to join your writing team.

The award that everyone seems to remember was the one from Mrs Mary Whitehouse's National Viewers' and Listeners' Association. Presumably we were selected for this publicity stunt because we were a nice, clean show. We wondered about whether to accept, and concluded that it wasn't up to us to approve or disapprove if her association liked our programme. Then we heard that Mrs Thatcher, who urgently needed a popularity boost, would be presenting the award. *Then* we heard that this was to happen live on *The World at One*. Finally, two days before the event, a scarcely believable message arrived from Number 10: Mrs T had written a *Yes Minister* sketch, which she intended to perform with herself playing the PM, Nigel as Sir Humphrey and Paul as the Minister for Administrative Affairs.

Phone lines were humming: Paul and Nigel both rang me, begging me to help them get out of this humiliation. I could do nothing; I explained that neither Tony nor I had been consulted, that they (the actors) had been asked and it was up to them to say yes or no. Though dreading it, they feared Prime Ministerial wrath even more, and with deep reluctance they agreed. The following day the script was rushed to Paul and Nigel, and copied to us. To say that it wasn't funny would be something of an understatement. We wondered if the Prime Minister had really found the time to sit down and write this crap, or whether her Press Secretary Bernard Ingham was the real author. Not that it mattered.[38]

The awful day dawned. We all went to the little church in Portland Place, beside Broadcasting House. The ceremony was to take place in a big basement room, which was packed with journalists and cameramen. There was a battery of mics and video cameras, the sort of thing you would expect at the end of a summit conference. The whole thing had been expertly timed by Bernard Ingham to be covered not only live on the radio but in the *Evening Standard*, on the evening TV news and in the following morning's papers. The sketch began, with everybody reading their lines rather badly: Mrs Thatcher couldn't act, and Nigel and Paul were reading badly in what looked like a half-hearted attempt to dissociate themselves from the whole embarrassing event. Then a strange alchemy occurred: it started to be funny just because, like Mount Everest, it was there. It was so ludicrous that we started laughing.

It was this sketch, seen by millions on the news that night, which gave rise to the legend that Mrs Thatcher had appeared in an episode of *Yes Prime Minister*. After it was over, Mrs Whitehouse made some brief remarks and presented the award itself. I can't remember what it actually was and I certainly don't have it on my mantelpiece, but after I was handed something I stepped forward to the mic. 'I'd like to thank Mrs Mary Whitehouse for this award,' I said, 'and I should also like to thank Mrs Thatcher for finally taking her rightful place in the field of situation comedy.'

There was a brief but audible gasp from the press and then

---

38 It can be read in all its frightfulness in *The Yes Minister Miscellany*, published by Biteback.

a volcanic eruption of laughter, one of the biggest laughs I ever got in my career. The room was rocking, everybody except one person: Mrs Thatcher. 'We are not amused,' her face plainly said. I was never invited back to Number 10 and never offered an honour, but the joke worked.

I used to say that it's okay to make a joke about anything. I still think that's true – but a joke is not good if it crosses the line from funny to not funny.

118. A few jokes are not worth the risk.

There was one subject that we never tackled, and that was the troubles in Northern Ireland. The basic joke was good and, as usual, was all about hypocrisy: Eire and the UK both pretended that they wanted Northern Ireland, but it wasn't true. The government of Eire didn't want responsibility for the Marxist provisional IRA, nor did it want to take on nine hundred thousand angry Protestants, many of whom were unemployed and violent; and the UK certainly didn't want the IRA nor the thousands of so-called loyalists who were only loyal when it suited them and violent when it didn't. Everybody but the Northern Irish wished that Northern Ireland would just sink into the sea and disappear.

This could have been the basis of a funny episode. The problem was: what if a bomb, set by either side, exploded and killed people the night the episode was broadcast? This would have caused the show to cross that line. It was a chance that we decided we couldn't take.

* * *

I was thirteen when I first saw Victor Borge at the Palace

Theatre in London. Without question, he was the funniest stand-up comedian I have ever seen, before or since. There was a moment when one man in the audience laughed loudly at something to which the rest of the audience did not respond. Borge fixed his piercing stare on that man. 'Sir,' he said, 'please be so good as to laugh with the rest of the audience. If you all laugh individually, we'll never get out of here!'

119. Comedy needs precision.

I saw Borge times over the years. His timing was immaculate and precise. Mark Twain said: 'The difference between the almost right word and the right word is the difference between the lightning bug and the lightning.'

One of the biggest challenges of comedy is that you have to make all the audience laugh *at the same time*. This is not an issue with drama. In drama, or tragedy, the audience can and will be moved to tears at different moments in the action. This is luxury that comedy is not allowed.

120. Comedies and horror films have something in common.

Consider the moment in *Jaws* when the audience first sees the shark. Spielberg wanted the whole audience to be scared out of their wits. He wanted the audience to scream all together. This moment is a perfect melding of both surprise and suspense. We have known since the beginning of the film that the shark is out there. We have seen the barrel that was attached to the harpoon, bobbing along on the surface. We surmise that the shark was angered by it. But Spielberg gets us used to the barrel and the shark's presence and he lulls us into a false sense of security. The boat is bobbing calmly on the surface, the tense music has gone, Roy Scheider is not even looking at the water – when suddenly, the shark attacks the boat. And we all scream. At the same time. Suspense and surprise. Masterly.

* * *

I have been fortunate to work with many precise comedy actors. Perhaps the most precise of all was the great Leonard Rossiter. In 1982 I was asked to write a short advertising film for Barclays Bank, starring Rossiter. I wasn't interested, no matter how much the producer Jeanna Polley offered, until finally my agent Anthony Jones rang me: 'She says, "What does he *want*?"' My thoughts were turning towards film directing, and I said I'd write it if I were allowed to direct it; Jeanna and Barclays both agreed.

I struggled with the writing; it was difficult to combine the advertising message and the comedy, but everyone liked the eventual script and it went rapidly into production. I called it *Mick's People*. We shot for seven days. Roger Pratt, now a celebrated director of photography, was the DoP and camera operator and I learned a lot from him. Leonard was the most brilliant and gifted actor with whom I'd ever worked, but not the easiest. He was surly and hostile and, when he left after six days, the rest of the cast ordered champagne to celebrate that they wouldn't have to work with him on the last day.

In spite of my inexperience, the film turned out well and subsequently won several first prizes at assorted advertising festivals. I swore, however, that I'd never work with Rossiter again. I was not expecting this phone call from Ray Cooney,

Director of the Theatre of Comedy, a year later: 'We're producing *Loot* with Len Rossiter starring, and he wants you to direct it.'

'No,' I said to Ray, with absolute certainty. 'You must have made a mistake. We didn't get along when we last worked together. He must mean some other Jonathan. Try Jonathan Miller.'

Five minutes later he called me back. 'No,' he said. 'Leonard wants to do it with you!' I had a long think. He was perfect casting for Inspector Truscott. The play was brilliantly funny. How bad could it be for three or four weeks? I said yes, but with serious misgivings. I treated Leonard with kid gloves. He didn't have casting approval in his contract but I gave it to him anyway, so that he would be involved in every casting choice and couldn't later turn on me to demand, 'Why did you cast that *amachewer*?' Amateur was one of his most derisive insults, which he pronounced 'ama-chewer' in a tone of dismissive contempt.

It was easy to earn Len's contempt: just make one mistake and there you were! Unless, that is, he liked you. His loyalty was as intense as everything else about him. He was a wound-up rubber band. Spiky, angular, shoulders hunched and tense, determined to be faultless at everything, he played squash and at the age of fifty-seven came third in the British Championships for the over-forties. He was a wine fanatic too – every cupboard in his house in Fulham was full of wine and temperature-controlled, each at a different temperature appropriate for red wine, white wine, champagne and so forth. Len and his delightful and patient wife, the actress Gillian Raine, invited us for dinner, and the evening began at the top of the house with some white wine or other. Len described it in some detail, in flowery wine language; I thought he was joking, but he was deadly serious. He poured the wine, we all held it up to look at the colour, we sniffed the bouquet; we sipped it and swirled it around our mouths, activating all the taste buds. That is, everyone except my wife Rita, who tasted it immediately, liked it and drank it pretty fast. 'That was lovely, Leonard,' she said. 'Can I have some more?'

His long ferrety face stared at her, aghast, his mouth in that famous thin-lipped sneer, his eyes small, furtive and mean. 'More?' he said. 'Already? This is fine wine, you're supposed to *savour* it, taste it, treat it with respect. You're not supposed to swill it down.'

Rita was unmoved. She is a psychoanalyst and had worked at Broadmoor, the top-security hospital for the criminally insane. She smiled. 'There wasn't such a lot in the glass. Now shut up and give me some more.' Len chuckled appreciatively, enjoying that she wasn't intimidated by his bluster. Rita had passed the test. He poured her some more and loved her from then on.

With Leonard's enthusiastic approval, I cast Gemma Craven, Patrick O'Connell (with whom I'd worked at the Belgrade in Coventry) and two young actors, Neil Pearson and David John. I consulted Len about the schedule. 'Would you like four weeks' rehearsal? Or five?'

'Five weeks?' he yelped, in horror. 'Fuck me! We'll go out of our minds with boredom. How about two weeks?' We settled on two and a half.

He wanted to talk about the set. 'There will be doors, right?'

'Of course there'll be doors,' I said. 'It takes place in a room.'

'So does *Tartuffe*,' he retorted. 'But when I was in it, it was all artsy-fartsy. The fuckin' amachewer who directed it thought he was very avant-garde and I had to walk forty feet from the wings to make an entrance. Killed every fuckin' laugh.'

I showed Len the model of Saul Radomsky's excellent set for *Loot*. With doors. He relaxed slightly, but not for long. Relaxation wasn't his thing.

Len knew virtually all his lines on the first day. Nobody else did. I told them to get cracking:

121. You can't rehearse farce or any physical comedy with the script in your hand.

Rehearsals were serious and tense: when Len wasn't in a scene he would pop down to the stalls and sit next to me, whispering questions about why they *still* weren't doing something I'd asked them to do. 'Not everyone's as quick as you,' I whispered back. 'It takes them time to think about notes and assimilate them.' Len couldn't see why. He didn't know why the young actors hadn't learned the lines in advance. He was in such command of his technique that there was never a question of *how* to do something; the question was, simply, which was the most effective choice to make. Then he did it at once. He was a virtuoso player of his instrument: himself. On the rare occasions that I thought of something he hadn't, he was slightly miffed; he felt he had been caught looking like an amachewer.

One day, as he sat beside me in the stalls, muttering in my ear, I suddenly became exasperated with him. 'Look, why don't *you* direct it?' I said. 'Why don't you just go ahead and tell them what you want? See what happens.'

He actually looked abashed. 'I did direct a play once. It was a disaster.'

'Why?'

'I couldn't see why they couldn't just fuckin' *do* it.'

Rehearsals were brief. Just over two and a half weeks, 10.30 to 4.30. Lots of time at night to learn the lines. Little time wasted gossiping or chatting. Total fierce concentration, doing tricky scenes again and again until they ran like clockwork. Gemma, an excellent dancer and singer, was accustomed to precision rehearsals. Paddy O'Connell was having a ball. The two younger actors didn't know what had hit them. This wasn't how they'd been taught to go about it in drama school. 'No Method shit here,' Len had remarked firmly.

122. Dramatic irony will make most scenes funnier.

Dramatic irony is when the audience knows more about the plot than one or more characters in the scene. It helps us perceive Oedipus as a tragic figure because we understand, long before he does, that he is the cause of the plague on his city. It adds macabre humour to King Duncan's entrance into Macbeth's castle: 'This castle hath a pleasant seat,' he says cheerfully, not knowing that his host and hostess plan to murder him that night. And dramatic irony adds big laughs to comedies. In *Loot*, for instance, Inspector Truscott picks up off the carpet a small round object that looks a bit like a marble. But it isn't. We, the audience, know that it's a glass eye from a corpse hidden in the house. Truscott looks at it, sniffs it, and then – cautiously and tentatively – licks it. The audience is simultaneously disgusted and convulsed with laughter.

But they would not laugh at all if, like Truscott, they didn't know what it was. The laugh is entirely due to the dramatic irony.

Many plays and films rely on dramatic irony throughout. All 'drag' films and plays, for instance, from *As You Like It* and *Twelfth Night*, to *Charley's Aunt*, *Some Like It Hot*, *Tootsie*, *Nuns on the Run* and *Mrs Doubtfire*, depend on the audience knowing something that other characters do not: that the leading characters are not the sex that they appear to be.

Dramatic irony even works in stand-up if a joke implies that the comedian doesn't understand what we the audience can see only too clearly. Bob Monkhouse did that really well: 'They all laughed when I said I'm going to be a comedian when I grow up. They're not laughing now.' And again: 'When I go, I want to die peacefully in my sleep, like my father – not terrified and screaming like his passengers.' (These are also 'tip-of-the-iceberg' jokes, Rule 69, in that they reveal a lot about the character of the speaker.)

Alfred Hitchcock loved dramatic irony. That is why he called his films *suspense films*, not thrillers and not mystery films. He disliked whodunnits because, as they are mysteries, by definition the audience knows less – not more – of what is going on than the detective protagonist. Furthermore, they all have to conclude with a lengthy explanation of who did it, with what weapon, in what room, and why – shades of *Clue*, which parodies those interminable explanations on *Poirot*, *Miss Marple* and all the other posh BBC detective series.

Hitchcock, on the contrary, always makes sure that the audience knows who the villain is; frequently the audience is told within the first ten minutes, but never later than halfway through the film. In Spielberg's *Jaws*, as we discussed earlier, the audience knows about the shark from the beginning, and yet the suspense is maintained for two hours.

Hitchcock valued suspense much more than surprise. If, for instance, a bomb is to explode, you can get one big and possibly scary jolt if the audience has been kept in ignorance. The better alternative, in Hitchcock's view, is to show the bomb being assembled, to show how dangerous a task that is; show the timer being attached and set, show it being put in a briefcase, carried to a car, being driven to the destination, being picked up from the car, carried into a room, placed under the table close to the target, and all the while these shots of the briefcase get closer and bigger, with huge close-ups of the timer as it approaches zero – and then, at the last minute, just as it is about to explode, a surprise: the person who is being targeted suddenly stands and moves away from the bomb to the furthest part of the room. Then it explodes.

Instead of two seconds of shock, this approach may get you ten minutes of suspense, with the audience on the edge of their seats, fearful, sweaty hands – and there is still a shock at the end of it.

Dramatic irony makes both genres work, suspense and comedy. In comedy, the more information the audience has about a scene and the less information one or more of the characters in the scene has, the funnier it will be.

123. Perfectionism can be irritating but it is necessary.

It became clear that, in *Loot*, Leonard was going to give one of the greatest performances of his extraordinary career.

For Truscott's first entrance, the front door faced directly downstage and was made of frosted glass so that his shadowy outline was visible. When the bell rang, one of the young men ran to the door, opened it, and on seeing Leonard immediately slammed it in his face, giving us a fraction of a second to catch his expression. It got a big laugh at the previews. On one of the late previews the door bounced open again.

Leonard was livid. After the performance he excoriated the designer, the stage management and the master carpenter. I told everyone it had to be fixed by the following morning, as if they didn't know already.

The next day I came in early. The door was fixed. I tested it ten times, slamming it hard. It stayed shut. Len came in, walked straight onto the stage, opened the door and slammed it. It stayed shut. He did this twenty times. It still stayed shut. On the twenty-first mighty slam, it bounced open. Len turned to me with a combination yelp and snarl. 'You said it was fixed.'

'It has been fixed,' I said. 'You were doing your absolute best to make it bounce open.'

'This has got to be a door that *never* goes wrong.'

'There's no such thing. Not the way you slam it.'

'Fuckin' amachewers,' he muttered as he stalked off to his dressing room. Things had to be *right*. He's the only actor I've ever seen standing on the street outside the theatre after the first dress rehearsal at midnight, actually checking the size of his name on the bill with a ruler, to make sure it was the size specified in his contract. Yet, after the show, unless we were going out to dinner, he caught the bus home to Fulham in spite of his great fame and instant recognisability. No fuss, no pretension, no chauffeur-driven car.

Thelma Holt, the producer, decided to decorate the Ambassador's Theatre in the funereal spirit of the play. *Loot* is another farce about death. The auditorium was draped with black crêpe. Sombre organ music played on the way in, not just in the auditorium but also in all the corridors. On the opening night, in keeping with the corruption in which the play delights, Thelma slipped a brown envelope full of cash to each of the critics as they collected their tickets. (Sadly, it was counterfeit.)

Leonard and the whole cast excelled themselves on the opening night and it was a smash hit. I was full of respect for his search for perfection, his absolute dedication to giving the best possible show to the audience at each and every performance. He sat in the wings from the 'beginners' call (five minutes to curtain up) even though he didn't appear for about fifteen minutes. He listened to the audience coming in, sizing them up. When the play began, the pace was often uncertain, sometimes a little slow, sometimes a little rushed; but within twenty seconds of Len's first entrance the pace stabilised at exactly the right tempo for that audience and stayed perfect for the rest of the evening. He was a magician with his timing.

His obsessive-compulsive attitude was a part of his whole life, and like all his friends I was now quietly amused by it. We had become pals; he adored Humphrey, our bearded collie (named after Sir Humphrey, because he was sound), and all trace of Len's brusque manner vanished completely when he was with our son Edward, aged nine, with whom he chatted easily and without a trace of condescension. We had many hilarious, noisy, politically argumentative dinners, and I particularly remember one with Bernard and Carol Donoughue where the discussion became so tempestuous that Rita ran out of the room, returned with a referee's whistle and blew it!

Everyone stopped shouting and turned to look. Rita said, 'From now on, you each get two minutes, then I blow the whistle and it's somebody's else's turn.' Eager to continue the argument, everyone instantly agreed to the rules. Len started. At two minutes Rita blew the whistle; being the expert comedian he was, he stopped mid-word and got a big laugh from the room. I had grown to love this impossible, brilliant man. I looked forward to doing another show with him. By the time *Loot* concluded its season at the Ambassador's it was clear that it could have run for years. Len had a new series of *Rising Damp* to do, so it was agreed that we would reopen *Loot* at the Lyric, on Shaftesbury Avenue, after that.

* * *

Tony and I set about writing the first series of *Yes Prime Minister*. I was on top of the world: *A Little Hotel on the Side* was a hit at the National, *Loot* reopened at the Lyric to great reviews and was playing to capacity, and writing with Tony remained tremendously pleasurable. Things were too good. One night, Rita and I went to the cinema and returned home to a message on the answering machine from the company manager of *Loot*; it said, 'Jonathan, Leonard died tonight during the performance, in the middle of Act One. Can you come to the theatre when you get this message as we're all still here and there are a lot of press outside?'

There were no mobile phones then, so we didn't get the full story until we got to the theatre. Leonard had played his first scene perfectly, as usual, and returned to his dressing room. When he was called to the stage for his next scene, he didn't come. The stage manager hurried to the dressing room and saw Len sitting up, at his dressing table, stone dead. They lowered the curtain, made an announcement that Len had been taken ill, and resumed shortly afterwards when the understudy was ready to go on. At the end of the show the cast, stricken, just sat around, waiting for the press to disperse from outside the theatre, talking about Len. Like me, they had all come to love him. Rita and I said what we could, but what was there to say?

He had had a bisecting aneurism and died almost at once, so quickly that he remained sitting in the same upright position in his chair. All I could think of at first was that he shouldn't have died – he was careful about what he ate, he was rail-thin and he exercised with religious fervour.

Grief overwhelmed me. I had only known him three years, and for the first two I hadn't even liked him, yet somehow, inexplicably, he had suddenly become a close friend. Now that he was gone, I missed him more than I could explain. I wept for days. Maybe it was the shocking suddenness. I believe it was Nancy Banks-Smith who said once that you measure the greatness of an actor by the gap they leave when they die; who, for instance, is there to play a Walter Matthau part? By that measure, Len was one of the all-time greats; time and again since he died I have realised that there was, and is, nobody like him.

While trying to deal with the horror that engulfed me at the funeral, I heard from Gillian, who wanted me to give the eulogy at his memorial in St Paul's Church, Covent Garden. Surely there were older, closer friends? But Gillie felt that this was what Len would have wanted, and I realised that he must have experienced our odd friendship in the same way that I did. I was moved, but it gave me a huge problem: what could I say? It's customary to say nothing but good things about the deceased, but I couldn't very well stand up and talk about how easy he was to work with or to get along with. Everyone would know I was lying.

So I talked about him as a perfectionist. This is part of what I said:

The thing about Leonard was that he could never pretend. He was unable to ingratiate himself with anyone. And truth is what art is about. An actor is searching for truth in his way, no less than a philosopher. Leonard constantly searched himself for the truth of every tiny moment in his performances and, in the process, that imitation of life by a great actor becomes a criticism of life, a search for honesty and illumination of how people behave in crisis, in adversity, at high and low points in their lives . . .

Some actors have been described as an ornament to their profession. Leonard was certainly no ornament. But he was a beacon: a light to guide the profession, a shining example of sheer professionalism and expertise. Leonard knew how to conceal the art. He made comedy look easy. Letting the audience see the wheels turning was the mark of an amateur, the worst thing he could say about anybody. He not only demanded perfection of himself, he demanded it of others. If this was not possible, then at the very least they had to do their best. That was his compromise. Those of us who took up the challenge, with all the attendant risks of failure, loved him for the inspiration and the target that it gave us.

'Even God can't work miracles,' says Inspector Truscott in *Loot*, and even God can't bring him back. God, with His usual arbitrary, undemocratic, high-handed, non-consultative approach to decision-making, has deprived us of Leonard. Perhaps God knew what He was doing. He is reputed, after all, to move in mysterious ways. But I hope He knows what He's in for. Now that Leonard is up there, things had better be properly managed: I hope that the Heavenly Gates opened on cue and that the Choir of Angels is singing in tune. They had better be professional in Paradise. Because, if not, they'll certainly hear about it from Leonard.

In that final paragraph the congregation laughed a lot, not just out of recognition of the truth but also, I think, out of relief that I had managed to pay tribute to him without lying. I was certain that Len would have been delighted. Writing that speech somehow helped me to come to terms with his death. Though he died nearly thirty years ago I still miss him. And I still wonder what really killed him. I believe it was all that anger which he couldn't quite repress, and which made him so funny.

124. Polish the dialogue until it sparkles.

From the writer and director's point of view, precision means that you must polish the funny moments until they shine. These may be in the dialogue or the action. Remember that great dialogue, though it may seem realistic, seldom is. It requires artistry, impeccable phrasing, the perfect vocabulary for the character, and the script should sustain a level of wit (whether or not the characters are aware of it) that is not possible in real life.

125. If you are making a film, more polishing should be taking place in the cutting room.

Alfred Hitchcock, a master of comedy as well as suspense, said that drama is life with the dull bits cut out. A comedy is life with the dull bits cut out *and* the wit and humour maximised.

The dull bits are often found in 'shoe leather'[39] or in the dialogue.

126. In a play or film, dialogue should be wittier or funnier than most of us could come up with in real life.

Why? Because it is more entertaining, and because through drama, tragedy or comedy, the audience enjoys living vicariously. If they're watching a comedy, the audience enjoys feeling vicariously witty.

* * *

In 1975 I read the script for *Bar Mitzvah Boy*. They were interested in me for the part of Harold, the bar mitzvah boy's sister's boyfriend. Harold was a true schlemiel, a nothing. Kind-hearted and well-intentioned, he was without courage or opinions and essentially agreed with whoever spoke last or loudest. A boring, uninteresting, forgettable person, without drive or initiative, he represented a fascinating challenge to play. Of course, Jack Rosenthal had achieved the near-impossible and written this completely bland character with such wit and observation that he jumped off the page. Harold, scared to offend anyone, had some wonderful tip-of-the-iceberg lines, like when he said to two characters who were flatly disagreeing with each other: 'I agree with you both. Wholeheartedly.'

After eleven years as an actor, during which all my TV

---

39 'Shoe leather' is film terminology for unnecessary shots of characters walking from one place, or one part of the set, to another. It also applies to shots of people driving from A to B. Such shots should only remain in the film if they reveal or intensify information about the characters or the situation. Or if you are making a European film.

appearances had been in situation comedies (*Doctor in the House*, *The Liver Birds* and *My Brother's Keeper*) and sketch shows (*The Dick Emery Show*, *Twice a Fortnight*), plus the odd small part in various drama series, it would be my first TV appearance in a single play. And Jack Rosenthal was an important writer. The part wasn't very big, but Rita encouraged me to go for it.

I went to the BBC TV Centre to audition for Rosenthal and the director, Michael Tuchner. Michael was a jovial person. Jack was quiet, watchful and dry. He had thick, wavy brown hair brushed back from his forehead and big glasses with thick brown frames. He chain-smoked all through my audition, and for the next twenty-five years. He was the man you wouldn't notice in the crowd, but he would have seen everything.

I don't think I impressed Michael Tuchner particularly, but Jack smiled and chuckled and said goodbye to me with great warmth, and I got the part. Four weeks of sheer joy resulted. There is nothing on earth like the fun of playing a part that you really know how to play. I understood Harold so completely that I could play it any way the director requested and *still* be him.

At the read-through one or two of the actors paraphrased some of the lines, and afterwards Jack made a speech, letting everyone know that he had spent much time and given much consideration to every word of the dialogue, and that it was not to be changed without his approval. Jack had no time for actors who turn up at the read-through, having read the script once or twice at home, and change dialogue with the lazy excuse, 'I wouldn't say that.' This happened at the read-through. 'You might not say that,' Jack said, 'but you're not the character. You're an actor playing this character, who

would say that. I know, because I wrote her.' I wanted to applaud.

127. Always have a read-through, especially for a film.

The read-through performs a variety of functions: it enables
the writer, director and producer to hear the whole thing
and to get an early impression of where it might need to be
tightened or improved. These early impressions are not always right, of course, and should be viewed with caution.

Some actors don't read the whole screenplay. At least, not
carefully. They only read their own part.

128. A read-through is the only way to be sure that all of
the cast have read the whole script.

A read-through also means that everyone meets, before filming begins. On my film *The Whole Nine Yards*, Harland Williams was unable to come to the read-through, so he and
Rosanna Arquette had not met before their first scene together. At 7am one chilly morning I introduced them:
'Rosanna, this is Harland. Harland, this is Rosanna. Now,
there's the bed, get into it, Harland, lie down, and Rosanna,
I'd like you on top, please.' This is not conducive to the best
acting.

129. A paradox: if you want to write something
universal, write something specific.

Look at *My Big Fat Greek Wedding*; not a great film but a colossal hit. Look at *Three Sisters* and *Uncle Vanya*.

Bar Mitzvah Boy was not expected to be a big success. We

thought it would mainly interest the Jewish audience, and not all of them would like it. The second part of that prediction proved correct, but not the first. It opened the *Play for Today* season of 1976 and was a hit throughout the country. Jack, as he did so often, had struck a universal chord. It went on to win the BAFTA Award – incidentally, beating *Ready When You Are, Mr McGill*, another wonderful play of his which was nominated in the same year.

As if that wasn't enough, this was one of three plays of his that won the BAFTA Award for three years in succession, an achievement that will probably never be equalled. The others were *The Evacuees* (1975) and *Spend! Spend! Spend!* (1977). He learned his trade writing nearly 150 episodes of *Coronation Street*, in its greatest days. What all his plays had in common were his great personal qualities – generosity of spirit, warmth, empathy, humanity – which shone out of all his work and made it accessible to everybody.

After *Bar Mitzvah Boy*, Rita and I had dinner with Jack and his wife, a brilliant and funny young actress called Maureen Lipman, who had starred in *The Evacuees*. We met his elderly mum Leah, known by her childhood nickname of Lakey. A few weeks later, on Rita's birthday, we were just sitting down in our kitchen to eat an undersized roast duck that had shrunk even further in the oven, when the doorbell rang. Jack and Mo stood there. They'd come from the hospital. 'Lakey died,' he said quietly. They came in and shared our infinitesimal duck; we celebrated Lakey's life and Rita's birthday, and we laughed and cried together. Somehow, that night, I felt I'd acquired a brother, only better.

After that, we all had brunch together virtually every Sunday for ten years: bagels, smoked salmon, cream cheese and endless cups of tea. We solved all the world's problems every Sunday morning. Nobody was listening, but we didn't mind. Jack loved pottering around in the kitchen. He was the rock in the centre of the household. He liked staying home; he worked there, and only went out when he had to. He didn't like to lock himself away to write, he liked to work with the family bustle all around him. He loved to make 'chopped and fried' (fried *gefilte* fish), with chips, bread and butter, and more tea.

130. You can base characters on people you know – they seldom if ever recognise themselves in a fictional script.

Jack suffered writing blocks from time to time, one of which, when writing *Bar Mitzvah Boy,* was connected with the character of Grandad. Then, one day, he was over at the house of his friend David Swift when he noticed that David's elderly father had a curious habit. Whenever anything was a cause for concern in that household he would recite a little poem in his quavery voice:

> *Our entry to it is naked and bare,*
> *Our journey through it is full of care.*
> *Our exit from it is God knows where –*
> *So if we're all right here, we're all right there!*

Every time David's father said this meaningless little rhyme, Jack noticed that the kids rolled their eyes and mouthed along with it. This is *great*, thought Jack. This is Grandad! He wrote it into the script and thought no more about it until, on the day that it was to be broadcast, David Swift phoned up. 'Good luck, Jack,' he said. 'We're all going to be watching tonight – me, Paula, the kids, my dad . . .'

His dad? Suddenly Jack was in a panic. What would David's dad feel when he saw Grandad saying this little rhyme and being mocked by the other characters? Jack was mortified. He couldn't enjoy the show when he saw it that night. All he could think of was how terribly he must have hurt David's dad's feelings. He got no pleasure from all the excited phone calls he received after the broadcast. He got no pleasure from the good reviews the following morning. And there had been no phone call from David. Finally, late the next afternoon, David rang. 'We all loved the show,' he said. 'Congratulations.'

Jack hardly dared to ask, but he had to. 'Was your dad watching?'

'Yes, he loved it. And when Grandad said that rhyme, my dad turned to all of us and said, "You see? I'm not the only person who says that."'

Over these years Jack and I shared many experiences, professional and personal. We both suffered through new musicals at the same time. On the night that the musical of *Bar Mitzvah Boy* opened in London, Jack stood in the lobby welcoming his friends. The show had taken a couple of years to write, and rewrite, and rewrite and rewrite again, all at the behest of an inept director, and each rewrite made the show worse than before. Jack knew this, but he was a team player. On the try-out in Manchester the company performed every night and rehearsed changes every day, and the show slowly went downhill. Late one evening, Jack wandered sadly around the theatre – front of house and backstage – and everywhere he looked he saw huddled groups of actors, dancers and crew, all weeping from disappointment and exhaustion. Standing in the lobby of Her Majesty's that opening night, we wished him good luck. He replied in his deadpan way: 'It was no trouble.'

What made his writing so accessible? He didn't write about the mighty or the powerful. Though highly educated and without any chips on his shoulder, he remained at heart a champion of ordinary people. You didn't have to be famous or important for Jack to love you. He didn't write satire, he wasn't trying to change political institutions, there's no bile or hatred in his work. He extracted universal truth from little stories about real life. He was a superb miniaturist. He loved people's foibles, he had an unerring eye and an aversion to all clichés. The children in his plays are not those precocious unreal kids one sees in most shows – they're real, and funny, and serious, and sad. So are the grown-ups. Jack's work celebrates the small victories of humanity.

When Jack wrote *The Knowledge*, he asked me to play Ted Margolis. I was thrilled. The film, when shown, was much loved and has been seen on TV many times over the years, a favourite with London cabbies. For the next twenty years I never had trouble getting a taxi in London, no matter how late or how rainy. 'Do you know Willifield Way, NW11?' I would ask.

'You should know, mate, you did the knowledge,' was the common reply.

131. Sentiment and sentimentality are different.

Sentiment is honest. It is another word for 'feeling'. Two or three years before Jack died we had one of our Sunday brunches at the Rosenthals. They were now pretty rare because Rita and I were living in America. Suddenly Jack said to me: 'Here, come in the study, there's something I want to talk to you about.' I followed him across the hall and into his office where, surprisingly, he shut the door behind us. I had supposed that he wanted to talk to me about an idea for a play. Instead he hesitated and then said: 'It's just that . . . well, we don't see each other that often any more, and . . . well, I just wanted to tell you I love you.'

I was astounded. Jack was never sentimental. Affection and love were always expressed with irony. I realised that this was not sentimentality, but real, honest sentiment.

132. Sentimentality should be followed by a treacle cutter.

Sentimentality is to sentiment what melodrama is to drama. It is fake and it is imposed from the outside. It is not properly rooted in the characters or the situation. And it is how many, if not most, Hollywood comedies wrap up their story.

At the end of a sentimental scene, a treacle cutter is essential. A treacle cutter is the old gag-writers' term for a funny line that cuts through the sticky, saccharine, cloying feeling of sentimentality. It is useful even when the sentiment is real, because it can get us back from tears to laughter, and return us safely to the genre of comedy.

I didn't know what to say to Jack when he told me he loved me. I couldn't think of a treacle cutter. Rather lamely I replied, 'I love you too.' We stared at each other, smiling but embarrassed. Then he gave me a quick hug, stepped back awkwardly saying, 'Well, that's it then. That's all I wanted to say. Let's get back to the others.' Back in the kitchen both Maureen and Rita gave us curious looks. Jack didn't say anything so I didn't either. Later that morning, when he popped out for some cigarettes, Maureen said, 'What did Jack want to talk to you about?'

'He told me that he loved me,' I said. They gaped.

This was a while before he was diagnosed with the multiple myeloma that killed him at the age of only seventy-two. Perhaps he had a premonition. Perhaps it was just that you never know when you'll see your friends again if they live six thousand miles away. His sanity, his lack of pretence, his unselfishness and his lovable personality live on in our memories as an example to us all. Anyway, now he's gone, and with him an era ended, the era of the single TV play.

Perhaps because of our conversation that day, and my lame response, Jack was better prepared for what I think was his last joke. The day before he died he came up with the best treacle cutter I ever heard. A friend of his phoned Maureen at the hospital and asked if he could have a minute or two alone with Jack as there was something he wanted to say. The friend arrived, went into Jack's room, came out after two or three minutes, and left. Maureen went in to see Jack, who was at death's door.

'What did he want to tell you?' Maureen asked.

Jack said: 'He wanted to tell me that he loved me.'

Maureen said: 'What did you say?'

Jack said: 'Nothing. We just had sex and then he went home.'

* * *

After Peter Hall pretended he hadn't heard my idea for a tragic and comic *Macbeth*, I had to come up with something else. I proposed *Three Men on a Horse*. It was an endearing fable by the great George Abbott, one of the giants of American theatre. He had directed the original productions of *The Boys from Syracuse*, *Pal Joey*, *Wonderful Town*, *The Pyjama Game* and dozens of others, and he had co-written forty-seven Broadway plays, this one with John Cecil Holm. It was first produced in 1935; although occasionally revived in America, it had not been seen in London since 1936. My mother, who saw it at the Wyndhams when she was twenty-one, told me about it, remembering it as blissfully funny. I read it and loved it. It seemed the right moment to revive it: it was the centenary of George Abbott's birth and he was still alive.

The play is about a hen-pecked husband called Erwin who writes rhymes for greetings cards. He has a magic gift: he can pick the winner of any horse race. He never bets, because he knows that he would lose his gift if he made money from it, so he just picks them for fun. That was the absurd premise and, in accordance with Rules 77 and 78, the audience accepted it without question. One day, in a bar near his office, drunk and unhappy about his marriage, three tough gamblers discover his gift and kidnap him. With hilarious consequences, as they say.

Having obtained the rights from his agent, I phoned Mr Abbott in Florida, shortly before his hundredth birthday. I feared he would be gaga, but his wife answered the phone and told me that he was flying in from LA that afternoon.

'Could he call me back when he gets home?'

'No, he has a game of tennis as soon as he gets here.'

A couple of days later I spoke to him. He hadn't heard about the production, he said, but he was delighted it was happening. The last time he'd been in London was when he directed *On Your Toes* at the Palace Theatre, only three years earlier, when he was ninety-seven, the same year he got married for the third time.

I asked him a few questions about the play, which he answered with total clarity. Before we hung up I asked him if he had any general advice about the play. 'Yes,' he said. 'The fellow who plays Erwin mustn't think he's funny.'

133. Leading characters in comedy should not know they are funny.

This should be Rule 1 for actors. The actor has to know, of course – but the character must not.

134. The *Cinderella* Rule.

George Abbott had another rule, one that he considered all-important. I had asked him a fairly general question about the structure of the play. 'It's *Cinderella*,' he said. 'They all are.'

'All? You mean, all your plays are *Cinderella*?'

'No. All plays.'

'You're saying . . . all plays are *Cinderella*?' I repeated, unable to process this notion.

'Of course! What is *Cinderella*? She wants something. She can't get it. She gets it. She loses it. She gets it again.'

'But only comedies, surely,' I said.

'No. You remember that play, with the man, the quadraplegic, lying in bed, wanting to die?'

'*Whose Life Is It Anyway?*'

'He wants them to switch him off. They won't do it. They agree to do it. He loses in court. He appeals, wins and dies. *Cinderella*!'

I don't know if George Abbott was right that all plays have this structure but it can be a useful guide.

A few weeks before we were due to start rehearsing, Peter Hall asked me not to do the play. The other directors at the NT had read it and expressed doubts about it. Uncertain, I began considering other, more earnest plays at Peter's request. I called a meeting of the company, explained that Peter was very worried about the public perception of the NT at that time, and asked them how they really felt about *Three Men on a Horse*; I wanted to know if they'd be open to considering one of the other plays I had thought of.

They were appalled. They all loved the play and several of them said they had joined the company because they liked it so much and specifically wanted to be in it. They were dismayed at my lack of determination. Bolstered by their commitment, I told Peter and my colleagues that I was sticking to *Three Men on a Horse*. They weren't pleased. On the first day of rehearsal one of the other directors stopped me in a corridor: 'How did the read-through go?'

'Pretty well,' I said.

'I can't think why you're doing it. Such a dispiriting little play,' he said, and wandered away, shaking his head sadly.

Rehearsals were hard, partly, I think, because my indecision over the play had shaken my company's confidence in me.

135. The director is a parental figure.

Actors have to be able to play. That's why they were called players. That's why we act in a 'play' or a 'screenplay'. They have to be able to take chances – the director's job is to provide an emotional safety net, so that they feel free to take chances.

They can't play properly unless they feel free, and supported and admired, but within safe boundaries. Directors, old or young, are parental figures. And yet the director cannot just indulge them, because he or she has responsibilities to the play or the screenplay, and to whoever financed the show.

136. Whether consciously or unconsciously, directors need to understand projection and transference.

Everyone comes to the director with their anxieties: the writer, the actors, the producers, the crew, the financiers. *Everyone*.

Everyone wants you to share their anxieties, because then hopefully you will agree to what they want. So you have to be able to distinguish everyone else's projections from your own concerns. If you can't do that, you are no longer in control. And if the director's not in control, everyone else feels very unsafe – and playing becomes hard.

Everyone – in short – is unwittingly doing everything they can to make you lose control over events, to push at the boundaries, to challenge your authority – but they're all horrified if they succeed. Just like kids. Just like patients in therapy.

Everyone – directors, actors, writers – everyone in our business needs a unique set of personality *defects*:

You need to have a sufficiently strong ego that you're not destroyed by repeated public criticism, yet you have to be vulnerable enough to function as an artist.
You need to have the vanity to believe you are uniquely ac-

complished (pride!), yet you need the humility to learn from others.

You need to be able to endure endless rejection, and yet be utterly confident as soon as you do get a job.

You have to compete in a ruthless rat race in which it's every man for himself, and yet be a good team player.

This is a big collection of what the psychiatrist R. D. Laing called 'double binds'. The director has to take a disparate group of talented people, with these real problems, assess each person individually, and try to work out what will help each one of them to do their best work.

* * *

Like all farce, *Three Men on a Horse* required rigorous drilling to perfect every comic moment, and some of the cast found the process hard and me dictatorial. Furthermore, the brilliant Ken Stott was new to farcical comedy and had great difficulty in playing it at the necessary speed; he seemed to be in the grip of the dreaded Method Acting. We didn't play it fast enough at our first preview, and when the chips were down, Peter Hall became a totally practical and supportive producer. I had a lot of unnerving notes from other senior management, and I checked them with Peter. 'Ignore them,' he said. 'It's fine. It's good. Just get the pace up.'

To start with, I couldn't. But finally, after a late preview I managed to impress upon Ken the need for increased pace: I told him that his character was the engine that drove the play forward, and it was up to him; if he didn't get it moving the play would flop and it would be his fault. I have never spoken like that to an actor before or since, but some instinct told me that he was big enough to take it. Fortunately I was right; he took it to heart and that night he gave a dazzling perform- ance. The play soared. Recently, after almost twenty years, we had a drink together. 'You said something to me that I've never forgotten,' he told me. I wondered whether it had been good or bad. 'It was good.' He smiled. What I had told him was:

137. Acting can be easy, and it can be fun.

We had arranged to go on holiday the morning after we opened in order to escape the reviews, good or bad. By now I had learned that the pleasure comes from the work itself; success or failure cannot be predicted so the best thing to do is to disappear after an opening night.

But on our return I ploughed through them all so that I could phone George Abbott in Florida. They were excel- lent. I told him we were sold out. He was delighted. Then I headed for LA to work on a TV series starring George C. Scott, and soon after I arrived I ran into Harold Prince at Mr Chow's restaurant in Beverly Hills. I didn't know him well, but we chatted for a minute or two and then he said reproachfully: 'You know, it would be awfully nice if you could call George Abbott and tell him how well the play has gone. He hasn't heard anything about it.' Suddenly I under- stood why, when I first called him, he told me that he'd not heard anything about the production from his agent. It was a memory problem; he couldn't remember new information. I called him again and, once again, he was delighted to hear all the good news.

The play won Best Comedy in the SWET Awards (now called the Olivier Awards), and George Abbott won his last big award at the age of one hundred. I hope he was told several times. The award was gratifying, but not nearly as much of a surprise as it must have been to all my director colleagues at the NT. George Abbott died seven years later, just short of his 108th birthday, in the midst of dictating changes for a planned revival of *The Pyjama Game*. It was appropriate for the NT to honour his centenary, and I'm glad we did it.

138. Nobody knows how the audience will react to any play or film or joke.

On that occasion I was right. On others, I've been very wrong. Instinct and years of experience can give you excellent guidelines, but no one gets it right every time. I think this is why Cubby Broccoli, the producer of the James Bond films, said that you should always judge people by their best work.

139. Members of the cast don't usually care to take responsibility for the failure of a show. That's what the writer and director are for.

Years later, in 1971, Bob Chetwyn phoned: he was directing a revival of J. B. Priestley's *When We Are Married* on tour, planning to bring it to the West End. This Rolls-Royce of comedies contained eight or nine funny leading roles. He offered me the part of Gerald Forbes, the church organist, which was not one of them.

He was written like an 'Anyone for tennis?' juvenile, for which I could not have been less suitable. Bob wanted it played differently and I said yes, mainly because it was nice to be wanted and employed again. I was also attracted by the idea of working with three truly great comedy actors: Peggy

Mount and Hugh Lloyd as Clara and Herbert Soppett, and Fred Emney as Henry Ormanroyd.

Rehearsals were difficult as I tried to find what I call a coat-hanger for my performance. Bob wanted me to play the part as a nervous musician – a good idea for the play, but rather a stretch for the lines as actually written. Peggy was kindness itself, supportive and generous: she was the exact opposite of the roaring *basso profundo* harridan that she usually played. Together she and Hugh Lloyd, whom I loved and admired, were the perfect hen-pecked husband and bullying wife, broadly comic but utterly truthful.

Fred Emney was almost the last of a dying breed, a great music-hall comedian. A famous curmudgeon, he was a big man in every direction, with a gravelly upper-class British voice, several chins, front and back, and a scrubby little toothbrush moustache. He wore a monocle and always smoked a big cigar. This was his persona and he saw no reason to change any of it just because he was in a play. He spoke with the quiet, strangulated voice of a retired colonel and yet somehow – because of perfect diction and clarity – you could hear him at the back of the biggest theatres on the tour. His first appearance was the key to the whole evening, entering very slowly through double doors upstage centre: first the audience was given a profile glimpse of his big belly; then a glimpse of the cigar; then, when they were fully primed, he slowly hove into view. He moved, not towards me or Ruby the maid, but to downstage centre where, acknowledging the applause, he gave two little bows, one to each side of the stalls, and then one more to the dress circle. Then he turned to us and the play would restart.

If he received no applause, he regarded the evening as virtually over. He would turn upstage after delivering his first line and murmur to us: 'Don't know why I bother! This crowd's a complete fuckin' waste of time, pickin' their noses, scratchin' their arses, we might as well go 'ome now!' We had to say our lines to him while this muttered tirade was in progress, and when he got his cue he would up the volume, turn slightly towards the front, throw in his line so that the audience could hear it and then continue grumbling while we spoke our next speeches. It was rather off-putting.

Two weeks after we opened on the road we played the Grand Theatre in Leeds, Priestley's hometown. This was the test. Priestley was coming to see it. We didn't know yet if we would go to the West End. We all wanted to, of course, but Priestley had the right to say no.

It wasn't a particularly big or responsive audience that Monday night. He sat in a box close to the stage. We could all see him clearly, lit by the spill from the lights, his large, pale moon-face dour and glum, just like his photographs. He didn't even smile, not once. When the curtain fell at the end of Act One nearly everyone was in a panic. 'Priestley didn't laugh – Priestley didn't like it – Oh my God, what happens if he doesn't like it? – We'll never go to the West End – Priestley doesn't like it!'

Fred Emney didn't panic. He sat down on the sofa centre-stage, stuck his monocle in his eye, took his cigar out of his mouth and muttered, 'Well, all I can say is, if he doesn't like it, he shouldn't have wrote it.'

* * *

140. Remember the old English proverb: You don't buy a dog and bark yourself.

What does a director do? I can tell you what a director doesn't do. He doesn't demonstrate to professional actors how to act a scene. They would be insulted, and rightly so. Furthermore, there would be no point. Either you demonstrate badly, in which case they learn nothing; or you demonstrate well, which makes them feel redundant and useless.

The director doesn't write the script. (You may, of course, but not qua director, only if you are also the writer.) By the same token, the director doesn't light the film or the stage, nor operate the camera, nor design the sets, nor the costumes, nor compose the music. I don't even get the coffee (well, not usually).

The director makes decisions. It is an imaginative job but also an executive job. The director gives people incentives and encouragement. The director selects the script or the writer, chooses the actors and the key crew: set and costume designer, composer, lighting designer (or director of photography). With the production designer, the director decides how the settings and locations will look. Then, with the cinematographer, he decides on the shots. He is asked questions continually, and must either give answers or help those who are asking the questions to find the answers for themselves. Truffaut defined a director as 'a man who answers questions'. The director must concentrate for every second, otherwise he or she might miss something vital that may have been suggested tentatively or played only once, and might not be offered or revealed again.

141. The director's job is to *help* everyone else.

My job, as director, is to help the cast and crew offer up the best work of which they are capable. I must try to enable the entire group to be as creative as *they* can be. Cajole, sympathise, understand, push, demand or do whatever else seems necessary for them to be at *their* best. They all need something different, depending on their task and their personality.

Here are a few rules that apply specifically to filming comedy:

142. You must have lights in the eyes.

A famous cinematographer once said to me, 'Wide-angle lenses. That's how you shoot comedy. That's all I use.' What he meant was that by using wide-angle lenses you can get full-figure shots, big depth of focus, and slightly comically distorted close-ups. There's some truth in that, but why limit yourself? Many people believe that comedy should be brightly lit, even front-lit all the time. That's why so many studio comedies look so flat. I disagree with this view.

I think that you should shoot comedy exactly the way you shoot drama. You use the right lens for the right shot. Sure, if you want a full-figure shot (and some people are funniest when you see their whole body) then a wide-angle lens is your choice.

My rule is: the only thing that's different about shooting comedy is that you must be able to see the eyes, and there must be lights in them. That way, you can see the facial expression, which is essential. The rest of the shot can be as shadowy and moody as the scene demands.

However, that cinematographer was right about one thing:

143. You will get smaller and fewer laughs if they can't see your feet, in a wide shot or in the theatre.

The film critic Penelope Gilliatt interviewed Buster Keaton late in his life, and asked him why he had given up making films. 'It's the wide screen,' I recall him saying, though I may be paraphrasing. 'How can you be funny if they can't see your feet?'

The curious thing is that this rule applies not just to great physical comedians and action comedy, but to theatre dialogue as well. Every actor knows that you get a bigger laugh if the audience has a full-length view of you; if you are stuck behind a sofa or a desk, for instance, the laugh will likely be smaller than if you can get yourself in front of it. This problem is mitigated if the barrier between the actor and the audience is not solid; so, for instance, it's much better to be behind a table than a sofa or a desk.

If you are behind a chair or a podium you should make sure that your hands are visible, preferably on furniture itself that is creating the barrier. Visible hands on the podium seem to be a foot substitute. For some reason, the audience likes to see your connection to the floor. It seems to solve the problem. Who knows why?

144. The biggest laughs are frequently on the reaction shots.

Never forget to shoot the reactions to a scene from other characters who are present but not necessarily speaking.

Sometimes they have to be in a separate shot. Without these reaction shots, many scenes are not as funny as they could otherwise be.

The reactions of other characters or bystanders are the same as the audience's reaction would be. It's another aspect of owning up. These reaction shots give the audience permission to laugh.

145. You must be able to cut a joke that doesn't work.

This is relatively easy to do in a play. But in a film you will not be able to do it if you have shot a scene in one long, meandering, lingering, beautifully developing shot.

Many directors think that it's better to shoot fewer and longer takes. They don't like to 'cut it up' because they feel that somehow there is more artistry involved in long takes. This ignores the crucial role that cutting has in pacing a film. They should take a look at Hitchcock's *Rope* and read what he says about it in the book *Hitchcock, by Truffaut*. *Rope* is shot apparently without cuts, in a succession of shots that each last the length of a reel. Beautiful long takes. However, the film has little pace or energy, and Hitchcock conceded that it was an interesting experiment that he would never repeat.

Comedies must always be shot with the ability to make cuts. You need to shoot 'coverage', which means other angles of all or part of the action. This enables you to remove, in the cutting room, anything that isn't working. If you insist on shooting a scene in one long take with no coverage, you must at least give yourself one other shot to cut to if needed: I call it the dog in the fireplace shot. If the scene is on the beach, it's the seagull shot. If it's an exterior night scene, it's the owl shot. You don't have to use it, but you must have a way to take out a moment of

196

comedy that turns out not to be funny, and a way to shorten a scene if it seems too long in the final context.

146. The director's job is to see that everyone is acting in the same show.

Everyone must be playing in the same style. All too often, you see a performance that appears to be 'over the top', or another where the actor seems to be 'phoning it in'. Neither of the actors may be at fault; it is the director's job to make sure that everyone is acting in the same show. In Mel Brooks's film *The Producers*, if one actor played one moment small and naturalistically, the whole house of cards would probably collapse. But because everyone is over the top, nobody is. It is simply the style of the movie.

The great director Tyrone Guthrie said:

147. The director is an audience of one.

Though making thousands of decisions, dozens every day, put yourself continually in the position of the audience, try to remain objective and ask yourself at every rehearsal or after every take: Did that work?

And if not, what would improve it?

148. The second act should be funnier than the first act. If there is a third act, that should be short, and the funniest of all.

Otherwise you create expectations in the audience and then fail to fulfil them. They hate it when you do that.

149. The last part of every film and play is a race to the finish, between the show and the audience.

The show must get there first.

Watch out for scenes that appear to be the ending, followed by other scenes that appear to be the ending, followed by . . .

Too many false endings irritate audiences. They get it in their minds that it is just wrapping up, and then it isn't. This can kill you.

If your last good laugh is three minutes from the end of the play or film, try very hard to cut at least two of the three remaining minutes.

If it's a film, try to do that while it's still on the page; it's much easier than in the cutting room. If it's a play, try to make the cuts before rehearsals begin: actors, understandably, don't usually like having their lines cut; they feel deprived or they take it personally.

150. Leave them wanting more.

The oldest rule in vaudeville. Less is more.

And finally, 'You've been a wonderful audience.'

If you're going to say this kind of stuff, don't be seen reading it off an autocue visible to the entire audience, as I saw a famous singer do at a concert at the MGM Grand in Vegas.

Not unless you have a really funny treacle cutter.

Acknowledgements

I owe grateful thanks to the following people:

Dinah Wood at Faber and Faber, who suggested this book, asked me to write it, corrected lots of mistakes and gave me countless helpful comments and suggestions; Mark Lucas, my agent, for his tireless efforts on my behalf; Peta Nightingale, who works with Mark; my friends Geetika Lizardi, Indre Viskontas and Tim Hoare for reading the manuscript, checking mistakes and making suggestions; Dakin Matthews and Dick Clement, for each suggesting a rule; Peter Markham and the directing students at the American Film Institute, to whom I first talked about many of these rules; Steve King and Alex Holroyd at Faber; Neil Titman for his meticulous copy-editing; and above all to my wife Dr Rita Lynn, who taught me what little I know about psychology and psychoanalysis and who has tolerated, with *almost* infinite patience, living for forty-four years with someone who does comedy. Plus she makes me laugh every day.

ff

Faber and Faber is one of the great independent publishing houses. We were established in 1929 by Geoffrey Faber with T. S. Eliot as one of our first editors. We are proud to publish award-winning fiction and non-fiction, as well as an unrivalled list of poets and playwrights. Among our list of writers we have five Booker Prize winners and twelve Nobel Laureates, and we continue to seek out the most exciting and innovative writers at work today.

Find out more about our authors and books
faber.co.uk

Read our blog for insight and opinion on books and the arts
thethoughtfox.co.uk

Follow news and conversation
twitter.com/faberbooks

Watch readings and interviews
youtube.com/faberandfaber

Connect with other readers
facebook.com/faberandfaber

Explore our archive
flickr.com/faberandfaber